MEDITATION
for the MODERN
FAMILY

Quarto.com

© 2023 Quarto Publishing Group USA Inc.
Text © 2023 Kelly Smith

First Published in 2023 by Fair Winds Press, an imprint of The Quarto Group,
100 Cummings Center, Suite 265-D, Beverly, MA 01915, USA.
T (978) 282-9590 F (978) 283-2742

Fair Winds Press titles are also available at discount for retail, wholesale, promotional, and bulk purchase. For details, contact the Special Sales Manager by email at specialsales@quarto.com or by mail at The Quarto Group, Attn: Special Sales Manager, 100 Cummings Center, Suite 265-D, Beverly, MA 01915, USA.

27 26 25 24 23   1 2 3 4 5

ISBN: 978-0-7603-8214-1

Digital edition published in 2023
eISBN: 978-0-7603-8215-8

Library of Congress Cataloging-in-Publication Data available.

Design and Layout: Tanya Jacobson, @tanyajcbsn
Illustration: Esté Hupp

Printed in China

The information in this book is for educational purposes only. It is not intended to replace the advice of a physician or medical practitioner.

• MINDFUL IN MINUTES •

MEDITATION
for the MODERN
FAMILY

Over 100 Practices to Help Families
Find Peace, Calm, and Connection

KELLY SMITH

For Porkchop & Mila

Thank you for making me a mom
and awakening a joy in my heart
I never knew could exist.

Contents

Introduction

Writing this book was kind of like raising a child. It is a living, breathing thing that I put my heart and soul into, and I wasn't entirely sure how it would all turn out until the end. This journey had a lot of ups and downs, learning, and exploration, and I wouldn't have it any other way.

When I first began teaching yoga and meditation over a decade ago, it wasn't the in vogue topic that it is now. Meditation and mindfulness were things that hippie, earthy-crunchy people did, and if you ever heard about kids or families meditating together, it was probably that odd homeschool family that lived off grid, ate food from their small organic garden, and used reusable diapers. I did have those families in my classes, and I absolutely adored them! But other people came too.

I saw parents, primarily mothers, who were curious what yoga was, or kids that saw us practicing together and thought it looked fun. I even had librarians from the local library asking if I would do a mindfulness story time to help kids deal with their stress and worry. I realized that it wasn't that people didn't want to learn how to incorporate yoga and mindfulness into their lives but they just didn't know where to start. They were curious about what mindfulness was, how to practice it, why they should practice it, and how it could possibly help their kids and themselves cope with the stress of everyday life.

I can definitively say that mindfulness has a powerful effect on many, and it can be extremely beneficial for everyone. Still, many of us don't know where to start, especially when it comes to trying to fit a meditation practice into our busy lives as adults and parents and when we want to introduce these practices to our kids too.

Over the past ten years, I have had the pleasure of getting to do what I love as a career and share the practices of yoga and meditation with students whose ages range from just a few weeks old to ninety-two years old. I have led students in the womb and those in their favorite rocking chair with their favorite sweatshirt with all fifteen of their grandchildren's names on it.

In November 2020, I welcomed my first child into this world, who we lovingly call Porkchop. Since then my desire to explore the benefits of mindfulness and meditation in the family system has only grown, not to mention my need to personally meditate now that I am the mother of a toddler as well.

I am so grateful that you are here, turning these pages and taking this journey with me. Wherever you are, whatever you are doing, you are the best parent for your child and there is no one in this world who could do it better than you. I am so honored that you have let me be part of your family's mindfulness and meditation practice, and I hope you enjoy the journey.

How to use this book

This book was created by a parent, for parents. It is a collection of personal reflections, messages, guided meditations, and mindfulness practices for the whole family. In these pages, you will find over 100 meditation practices, 250 mantras, and insights into how to bring mindfulness and the practice of meditation into your life and household.

How you decide to approach this book is up to you. You might read this book from start to finish, taking in all the information at once, and then periodically return to the sections that are most relevant to you. You might review sections during times that they feel most relevant to you, or you might read just a little bit each night based on what you are feeling.

As a parent, you are the best teacher and guide, and you know what is best for you and your family. This theme will pop up time and time again as we explore mindfulness together, but I want to affirm it right here and now.

You know what is best for you and your family, including how you want to use this book.

This book is divided into five chapters. The first two chapters section will help you understand the foundations of meditation, get a crash course in mindfulness, explore how to set up a simple but effective meditation practice, introduce how to share mindfulness with your family, and explore the benefits of spending intentional time together as a family.

The third chapter covers thirty-three topics based on real-life challenges and needs of adults and children alike. Each section has notes and insights into that topic followed by three meditation practices—one for parents, one for adolescents, and one for the little ones in your life—plus five mantras for daily use. Although these practices are divided by age, anyone can use any of these practices. Follow your intuition, take the pieces that resonate with you, and leave the ones that don't.

The fourth chapter is for the growing family and has meditation practices for women who are trying to conceive or who are awaiting the arrival of their newest family member. You will explore how meditation can benefit you as you grow your family, as well as seven guided practices that I found to be particularly helpful, followed by forty mantras just for mama.

The final chapter features practices for partners to do together to foster closeness, teamwork, and connection as you raise children together, plus thirty mantras that will help to support the bond between you and your partner.

My hope is that this book will be there for you when you need it as you navigate the wild ride that is parenthood, with all its ups and downs. I hope it brings you peace of mind and gives you the tools you need to incorporate mindfulness into your family system and cultivate closeness and joy within yourself and your family.

CH 1

Meditation
101

What Is Meditation?

Before we talk about what meditation is, we need to talk about what meditation is not. Contrary to what you may think, meditation is not the same thing as mindfulness. It isn't a religious practice, and it isn't the practice of magically turning your mind off and being devoid of all thoughts.

Plain and simple, meditation is the act of single-pointed concentration.

One of my favorite ways to explain meditation is to talk about light bulbs.

Imagine that your mind is a light bulb. When you are walking around, living your life every day your mind's light is on, shining in all directions, illuminating all things around you. But when you sit down to meditate, you are turning that light bulb into a laser, and you are taking all of your mental power, or "light," and focusing it intently on one point of concentration, illuminating only that point and nothing else.

The point of concentration can vary from practice to practice. For instance, a point of concentration could be your breath, a mantra, a feeling, such as loving kindness, or even the words of a guide who is leading a visualization (like the ones you hear on my podcasts, *Mindful in Minutes* and *Meditation Mama*). Your point of concentration can be anything, but, for it to be meditation, you will only have one point of concentration at a time.

How does this differ from mindfulness?

Although the two terms are used interchangeably quite often, they are two different practices—related, but not the same. Think of meditation and mindfulness as cousins, not twins.

While meditation is the act of single-pointed concentration, the practice of mindfulness is doing any action or activity with your full attention and awareness. So if meditation is turning your mental light bulb into a laser, mindfulness is turning the light bulb up all the way up and letting it fully illuminate what is in front of you.

You can do anything mindfully—fold your laundry, go for a walk—as long as you stay fully present with that activity. Typically, it's not possible to meditate while doing something else.

This book includes both mindfulness and meditation practices and provides ideas on how you can use both practices to live a fulfilling and present life. It is my belief that the sweet spot lies in using both meditation and mindfulness: meditation to build your focus and concentration, and mindfulness to let you fully witness and engage with life from moment to moment.

Why is meditation a "practice"?

You may be wondering why it is called a meditation practice, instead of a meditation training session or something else.

We refer to meditation as a "practice" because it is a time for you to practice for the real deal—that is, everyday life. For example, if you are focusing on your breath during your meditation to help alleviate your anxiety, you are practicing how to use your breath in moments of anxiety that show up in your everyday life. Or maybe you are working with the feeling of forgiveness during your practice, in which case you are building your forgiveness muscle so that when life asks you to forgive, you have the tools to do so.

Meditation is designed to be an exploratory time. It is a time where you can observe what is happening within you and around you and focus on developing tools that will help you live with presence and patience.

Meditation asks us to be an observer of what is happening within us, and around us, without judgment. It teaches us how to objectively look at our lives, behaviors, thoughts and feelings and go deeper into the root cause of these experiences.

Is meditation a religious practice?

Although meditation has roots in religious practices—such as Buddhism, Hinduism, and Christianity—the act of meditation does *not* mean that you are practicing a particular religion. Meditation is practicing single-pointed concentration, and you can choose what that point of concentration is. This means that you could also use your meditation practice as a form of devotion and prayer, if that is what you choose to focus on during this time. But it could be anything else, too, like your breath or a mantra.

The Benefits of Meditation and Mindfulness

You likely have heard that mindfulness and meditation are good for you, but you may not know exactly how far reaching the benefits of meditation are. Meditation and mindfulness research is booming, and the results are exciting for anyone who meditates or works in the wellness space. Over the past few decades, pioneers in mindfulness research, such as Dr. Sarah Lazar, Dr. Judson Brewer, and Dr. Larissa Duncan, have been exploring how these practices benefit your body, mind, and emotional well-being.

Recent studies of mindfulness and meditation have shown that a regular meditation practice can:

- Boost your immune system
- Improve concentration, mental clarity, memory, and focus
- Decrease stress, worry, loneliness, depression, and anxiety
- Decrease blood pressure and improve overall heart health
- Improve sleep quality and duration
- Slow signs of aging, physically and mentally
- Decrease pain and inflammation in the body
- Increase self-awareness, positive thoughts, and positive self-talk
- Increase social connection, emotional intelligence, and kindness
- Improve your ability to regulate your emotions

To put it simply, meditation can help benefit your physical, mental, and emotional well-being, and it is a wonderful way to care for your body, mind, and heart.

Meditation and the brain

Perhaps one of my favorite parts of meditation is how it can physically change your brain.

When exploring how meditation changes the brain, we first look at the concept of neuroplasticity—the ability for the brain to change over time and reorganize neural pathways to form new connections. Your brain is constantly changing and evolving based on your environment.

Basically, your brain can and will change over time, when learning new things or if you are in a new or changing environment. Our brains are always growing, changing, and reorganizing. It's growth is impacted by what we do on a day-to-day basis. Incorporating a small habit like ten minutes of daily meditation can change your brain in profound ways.

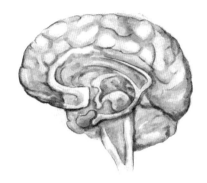

Harvard professor Sarah Lazar found in a 2011 study that regular meditation changes the size of many key regions of the brain.

What she found was that after about eight to ten weeks of regular meditation, the amygdala (the pain, fear, and worry center of the brain) began to shrink, while the prefrontal cortex (the memory, emotion, and productivity part of the brain) grew in mass and density. The latter region of the brain became thicker, and the number of the folds increased, meaning that there was more surface area for new neurons and for neurological activity to occur. At the same time, the amygdala would shrink or atrophy, meaning that smaller physiological responses to anxiety, worry, and pain would occur and participants would experience a reduction in the fight-or-flight mechanism within their body.

Psychiatrist and neuroscientist Judson Brewer found similar changes in a 2011 study looking at how the brains of long-term meditators are different from brains of people who don't meditate. In this study, Brewer reported that the brains of experienced meditators (those who had been meditating ten or more years) showed decreased activity in the areas linked to attention lapses, anxiety, attention deficit hyperactivity disorder, schizophrenia, autism, and plaque buildup in Alzheimer's disease. This effect was seen regardless of the type of meditation practiced, suggesting that any style of meditation will help you achieve these results.

Now, if you're worried about having to add thirty or sixty minutes of meditation into your daily routine to get these neurological benefits, don't. In a 2017 study performed at the University of Waterloo, researchers found that even ten minutes a day was enough to get the mental, physical, and neurological benefits of the practice, which means that a regular meditation can be a micro habit you can add to your life that will have a significant, lasting impact on your body and brain.

How to Meditate the "Right" Way

I get asked about meditation all the time, and one of the first things that people ask is if they are meditating the "right way." I want to clear something up right now. If you are meditating—that is, if you are practicing single-pointed concentration—you are meditating the "right way."

Meditation is a personal practice. It is, honestly, low stakes and should be fun and nourishing—something that adds value to your life. It is a way to alleviate your stress, not add more stress to your life because you're worried about if you're doing it right. When you try to focus your mental power on one thing, clear your mind, and become an observer of what is happening within you and around you, you are meditating.

Meditation will look different for everyone. We are unique individuals, and our meditation practice will be as unique as we are. Don't let worries about how to meditate stop you from practicing.

The next chapter of this book offers suggestions for how to set up a meditation practice, but just like in parenting, you know what is best for you. Feel free to explore, have fun, trust your intuition, and do what feels right.

What to do with distractions

One of the most common things I hear when I tell people that I am a meditation teacher is, "I tried meditation once, and I was so distracted! I just couldn't do it!" If you are someone who believes they are "too distracted" to meditate, that is like saying you're too dirty take a shower. There, I said it. If you are distracted in life, you could deeply benefit from a practice like meditation.

All jokes aside, as someone who has been diagnosed with clinical attention deficit hyperactivity disorder (ADHD), I completely understand how having a scattered mind and getting distracted easily can make the practice of single-pointed concentration challenging. But I also know first-hand how beneficial meditation can be if you struggle with a wandering mind.

Distractions can come in many forms, such as intrusive thoughts, itches, worries, external sounds, the urge to move, wondering if you remembered to unplug your curling iron this morning, or trying to write your grocery list in your mind for later.

Although distractions get a bad rap, I propose that distractions are a good thing. They are an important part of the meditation process. If you already have the power to focus non-stop on one thing indefinitely, what is the purpose of meditation? Treat distractions as an educational experience, building your ability to focus.

Your mind is like a stubborn toddler; it doesn't want to be controlled or told what to do. It wants full autonomy, living life in the driver's seat, with the foot on the gas pedal, careening over anything that gets in its way. When dealing with a toddler like this, how do you respond? Fight back and yell and cry just as loud as them? Force them to listen and focus? Scold them for acting like a child? No. You would be patient, wait it out, gently redirect, and send love their way.

If you think of your mind when you are extra distracted as a similar experience to those moments when your toddler has been captain of the hot mess express, it will help you to gently guide yourself back. Be patient and send love your way, just like you would with your child.

You can't stop your mind from thinking any more than you can stop your heart from beating or your hair from growing. It is going to happen. Our goal with distractions isn't to never have them again but to strengthen our ability, over time, to release your distractions and return to a point of concentration. Distractions will happen frequently and often. Maybe you will begin by getting distracted once every five seconds, or even once every two seconds. Maybe eventually you increase your length between distractions and only get distracted once every ten seconds, which, incredibly, is quite advanced.

The point of meditation isn't to remove all distractions but to improve your ability to come back when you inevitably get distracted. Distractions will happen. The test of your meditation practice is what you do when distractions happen. Welcome the distractions, embrace the struggle, and treat your mind like that turbulent toddler who needs to be gently guided back when it has wandered.

Tips for beginning a meditation practice

Although there is no one-size-fits-all approach to meditation, there are some ways that you can set yourself up for success when starting a practice. These are the tips that I share with my students to help them set up a realistic, sustainable, and enjoyable practice regardless of whether you're just starting out or you're looking to revamp your existing practice.

My top tips for building a simple and sustainable meditation practice

1 Find a teacher or practice that resonates with you. Try different ones until you find the one that feels right to you.

2 Be realistic about how much time you want to meditate (remember, ten minutes is enough!).

3 Choose a time of day that you are most likely to be consistent with your meditation practice. I usually recommend the first or last ten minutes of your day. Stay consistent!

4 Think of meditation as something that is contributing to your well-being rather than just another thing you have to do.

5 Find a comfortable meditation position that works for you. It doesn't need to be an easy seated position.

6 When you start a meditation practice, think about why you are starting this practice. Write down your why and put it near your favorite meditation space to remind yourself why you carve this time out for yourself each day.

Do I have to sit on the floor?

Contrary to common belief, you do not need to sit cross-legged on the floor to meditate. Although social media may suggest otherwise, you can meditate any way and any place that you find comfortable. When finding your meditation position, consider the following.

• Can you get comfortable enough that you won't be distracted by unnecessary aches and pains in your body, but not so comfortable that you may fall asleep?

• Can you breathe comfortably without anything interfering with your diaphragm?

• Can you create a long spine in this position and soften your shoulders?

If you are able to get comfortable, have a long spine, and can breathe without anything getting in the way, you have a good meditation position.

A few alternatives to sitting on the floor are:

- Sitting in a chair, with your feet firmly planted on the ground
- Laying down on a yoga mat or in bed
- Sitting on a meditation cushion
- Kneeling with a cushion under your knees

You don't need to make your body fit a meditation position. Instead, think about how you can make a meditation position fit your body.

CH **2**

Meditation
and the Family

How to Talk with Your Kids About Meditation

First, I want to remind you that you are the person who knows your child best and who understands what will resonate with them the most. Always trust that. That being said, here are a few tips on how to start talking to your kids about meditation if you want some guidance on that.

Start a meditation practice, and lead by example.

One of the best ways to open a conversation about meditation with your child is to let them see you meditating or exploring mindfulness in your everyday life. Be honest with your kids about why you meditate, how you do it, and what you feel like the benefits are. Keep it light-hearted and inquisitive. Let them explore, ask questions, and just chat. If they are curious, ask them if they want to join you for a meditation.

Ask your kids what they know about meditation.

Chances are your kids have already heard about meditation or mindfulness at school, online, or maybe even from their friends or other family members. So why not start the conversation by asking them what they already know? You might be surprised by how much they know about the practice already, and this might be the perfect way to suggest that you start exploring meditation together as a family.

Talk about the benefits of meditation for certain struggles.

If your child is struggling with something specific like anxiety or insomnia, or they struggle to speak kindly to themselves, try talking about how meditation can help. Share the benefits that you think will resonate with them the most. Letting your kids know how meditation can help them with a particular struggle in their life, backed up by facts and science, might be the open door you need to share this practice with them.

Start a new morning or evening routine.

If you are a family that loves traditions and routines, why not pitch the idea that you start a morning or evening meditation practice together? Make it fun, talk to your kids about the practice and why you want to do it, and let them be a part of the planning process when creating this new sacred self-care ritual for your family.

The Benefits of Togetherness

Some of the best memories are made when you are together with family. Claiming little moments of togetherness feels good and helps build the bonds between family members. Additionally, studies have shown togetherness to have the following benefits:

- Strengthened family core
- Improved academic performance in children
- Fewer behavioral outbursts
- Decreased risk of drug and alcohol abuse in children and parents
- Increase in individual happiness and confidence
- Reduced stress and anxiety

Togetherness can look like different things for different people. It can be family dinners, singing a special song before bedtime, or a daily meditation together—or something else. Have fun with it! You will get these benefits just by spending quality time together no matter how long or what you're doing.

Meditating as a Family

There are no hard and fast rules about how to meditate as a family or what this should look like in your household. Every family is different; each member of your family is unique and will want something different. Go with the flow and let your family explore mindfulness and meditation. This practice should always feel like something that is adding value to your life, fostering closeness, or bringing other benefits to your life.

Carving out time as a family can be a struggle, but eight to ten minutes a day of meditation is enough to get the mental, emotional, and physical benefits of the practice. While improving individual well-being, meditating together can strengthen family bonds. And it can be fun, an experience where you meet your children where they are at.

The next chapter offers nearly 100 practice ideas that incorporates the whole family. Consider these to be a starting point. Play around, try new things, create variations, and always do what feels best for you and your kids. Trust your gut, have fun, and enjoy mindfulness as a family.

*Meditation
Practices for the
Whole Family*

This chapter is the heart and soul of the book. It explores meditation topics as they pertain to parenthood and family. Each of these mini "meditation lessons" includes three guided practices, one for each of the different age groups in your family: Adults (ages 16+), Kids + Teens (ages 9 to 16), and Little Ones (ages 4 to 8). I've also included five mantras for each practice to help you further explore and connect to the subject at hand.

When I first began outlining this book, narrowing down the meditations for this chapter was hard! How could I ever decide on a handful of topics that would relate to parents and kids alike? With the help of my community, I came up with a list of ideas and challenges that occur most often for us as parents and for our children.

With each meditation topic, I share personal reflections and teachings from my experience as a mother and a meditation teacher. Then I give you practices to use for yourself and your family to engage with that topic. My hope is that these reflections will help you find moments of pause during the day and will support you as you walk the wild, winding path of parenthood.

If you're not sure how to share these meditations with your kids, this is what I recommend: For Kids + Teens, you can either guide older children through the practice by reading from the book aloud or hand them the book so they can practice on their own. For Little Ones, stay with the child through-out the meditation, guide them through the practice, and, in some cases, participate along with them. If your child can read, you can also have them read the instructions out loud and then you can practice together.

A Note on Mantras

This book includes over 250 mantras, and I want you to be able to use them to the best of your ability.

The word *mantra* is a Sanskrit term that means "sacred sound" or "sacred utterance." The word mantra can be broken down into two parts, "man" (or manas) meaning *mind* and "tra" meaning *tool* or *vehicle*. In essence, the word mantra means *a sacred tool* or *vehicle for the mind*. Mantras were originally used during a meditation practice to reach a higher state of con-sciousness or awareness.

The purpose of a mantra is to help you focus and deepen your meditation, while also facilitating inner peace and bringing you to a deeper understand-ing of the self.

A mantra can be one word (*om*) or a full-length poem or phrase. You can speak your mantras out loud or just repeat them in your mind, and there is no set number of repetitions you must do. Mantras are very intuitive tools, and they rely on vibration, intention, and the participant to bring power and meaning to the individual word or phrase to cultivate something specific into their life.

Each mantra is believed to have a distinct meaning, unique vibrational frequency, and intention, which is why some will resonate with you and some will not. This is also why I included five mantras per topic in this chapter. As you move through the sections, feel free to play around with all of the mantras, choosing whatever resonates with you on particular day. Trust your intuition, and use the mantras that feel right to you during your practice. You can even go off script and develop your own!

Breathing Techniques

Throughout this section, you will find several breath techniques that I return to again and again. These practices are extremely beneficial for your meditation practice and nervous system but can also be done as a standalone pranayama or breathwork practice. These breath practices are well suited for all ages.

Alternate nostril breathing

For this breath, you will use the ring finger and thumb of your right hand to alternate between opening and closing your left and right nostrils, inhaling and exhaling through the open nostril in a repetitive cycle.

- Bring your righthand ring finger and thumb up to your nose.
- Close the right nostril with your thumb and inhale through the left.
- Use the right ring finger to close the left nostril. Release the right nostril and exhale through the right nostril.
- Keep the left nostril closed with the ring finger and inhale through the right nostril.
- Then close the right nostril with the thumb, release the left nostril, and exhale through the left nostril.
- This completes one cycle of alternate nostril breathing. For a standalone practice, repeat this ten to twelve times, then release your hands to your lap and finish with three deep breaths through both nostrils.

Box breath

The box breath is made up of a 4-4-4-4 count.

- Begin by exhaling all the air out of your lungs.
- Then inhale for a count of 4.
- At the top of the inhale, hold the breath for a count of 4.
- Then completely exhale for a count of 4.
- When you have completely exhaled, hold the breath again for a count of 4.

- This completes one cycle of box breath. For a standalone practice, try box breathing for three to five minutes and visualize a box being drawn in your mind with each breath drawing one side of the box until it is complete after all four of the 4 counts.

Relaxation breath

The relaxation breath uses a 4-7 breath count.

- Begin by exhaling all the air out of your lungs.

- Then inhale for a count of 4.

- Pause for a moment, and then exhale for a count of 7. This completes one cycle of relaxation breathing.

- If you want to practice relaxation breath as a pranayama practice, try twelve rounds of this breath to quiet your mind and activate the parasympathetic nervous system.

Belly breath

Belly breathing focuses on sending the breath down low into your belly and minimizing any movement in this chest on each breath.

- Begin by exhaling all the air out of your lungs.

- Inhale deeply, feeling the rise of the belly.

- On the exhale, release your breath and feel the natural fall of the belly.

- Continue to breathe low, focusing on the rise and fall of the belly as you breathe in and breathe out.

- Belly breathing is a great practice for any time you want to return to the present moment, quiet the mind, or slow down your body and mind. As a standalone practice, try five minutes of belly breathing in a quiet space.

Three-part breath

Three-part breath works by inhaling in three short, consecutive bursts, followed by releasing all the air in one long exhale.

- Begin by exhaling all the air out of your lungs.
- Take a short inhale, filling your lungs about one-third of the way with breath.
- Take another short inhale, filling your lungs another third of the way.
- Take one final inhale that fills you up the final third, so you are completely full of air.
- Through slightly pursed lips, take a long, full exhalation.
- The pattern of this breath is in, in, in, out (long). This completes one cycle of three-part breathing.
- As a pranayama practice, do ten rounds of this breath followed by three deep breaths with your natural breath pattern.

Balancing breath

The balancing breath is a lot like Box Breath (page 32) but without the pauses at the beginning and end of the inhale and exhale.

- Begin by exhaling all the air out of your lungs.
- Inhale for a count of 4.
- Exhale for an equal count of 4.
- This completes one cycle of the balancing breath.
- As a pranayama practice, try doing balancing breath for three minutes.

Be Present

Perhaps starting this reflection with a gripe about unsolicited parenting advice is not the most graceful way to talk about being present, but in all honesty, this is what comes to mind when I reflect on how this topic pertains to parenthood. Since Porkchop was born, I've heard this one piece of advice time and time again: "Slow down, enjoy these days while they last because they go by so fast!"

Now, I don't know about you, but if I had a dollar for every time someone told me to enjoy these days and be present while out and about with my baby, I could have retired by now. The irony of how strangers were constantly telling me—a meditation teacher!—to slow down and be present wasn't lost on me. But I did struggle to see the humor in it at the time. It's hard to laugh when you're treading water.

Thinking back on the first few months of motherhood—a time marked by sleep deprivation and seemingly endless breast pumping—it felt like I was trying to keep my new life together by threads. So when I heard "slow down, enjoy these days!" from people whose children were grown, in all honesty, it kind of irritated me.

It didn't irritate me because they were wrong. It irritated me because deep in my heart I knew they were right. I could see myself living life with the fast forward button pushed down. It felt like I was on a rollercoaster, holding on for dear life, just waiting for the ride to end. One night, after what felt like hours of rocking Porkchop in the middle of the night, I finally laid down and all I could think about were the million other things that needed to get done.

At the same time, I was thinking about everything that I "should" be doing, but instead of doing those things, or sleeping—which was what I needed the most—I found myself laying in bed, missing my little guy. Although just a few moments ago my body was there rocking him, my mind was elsewhere, and it hit me like a breast pump to the face: these were the moments that people were talking about.

The late night snuggles, the quiet little coos of my infant as I change his diaper, the moments of just him and me that wouldn't be there forever. . . they were here *now* and I had the chance to be present and soak it up while I could. It was that night that I decided I wanted to consciously do my best to start slowing down and soaking up the moments and not just take photographs for later so I could remember these days in the future.

Being present is one of the greatest tools that you can use in your life and one of the greatest gifts that you can share with your child. Juggling life, being a parent, working, and everything else that you manage in this season of life is not easy. We live in a world that is filled to the brim with so much that the default is to be mentally elsewhere constantly.

When we slow down and focus on being present with ourselves, it allows us to really see how we are doing. It also allows us to be present in those special little moments with our children as they grow up. Being present asks us to be in the here and now with both our bodies and our minds, experiencing the moment for what it is: the good, the bad, the wonderful, and the difficult and everything in between. It asks us to slow down, open our eyes, and observe and witness life as it turns around us.

When life feels like it is moving at super speed, try these meditations to return to the present moment.

Meditation Practices for Being Present

For Adults

Take a moment to give yourself permission to slow down and be present.

Connect with your breath. Notice how you are breathing and begin to slow it down.

Send the breath into your belly and sit with the experience of breathing for a few minutes.

Check in with your body. How is your body feeling right now?

Check in with your mind. What thoughts are going through it today?

Check in with your heart. What feelings are you experiencing today?

Open your senses and experience the moment as you breathe. What do you hear, feel, and think about what is happening right now in this moment?

Sit, breathe, and be present in this moment with your body, mind, and heart and for at least seven minutes.

For Kids + Teens

Begin by taking three deep breaths. Inhale through the nose and sigh it out through the mouth.

Remind yourself that you are checking in with how you're feeling today without judgment.

Find your natural rhythm of breath, and follow your breath as it moves in through your nose, down your throat to the lungs on the inhale, and how this process reverses itself on the exhale.

Imagine the breath is your favorite color. Watch it flow in and out of your body from your nostrils. Do this for five minutes.

End your meditation by telling yourself three times, I am present in my body, mind, and heart.

For Little Ones

This practice can be done inside or outside, and your little one may benefit from doing this practice with an adult for extra guidance.

Have your child take a moment to get comfortable, close their eyes, and settle in. Instruct them to connect with their breath, have them slow it down, and guide them through taking five deep breaths.

Now call out each of their senses and begin cycling through them. Ask your child: What do you hear? What do you smell? What do you feel? What do you see? What do you taste? Have them answer out loud as you ask these questions.

Continue to cycle through the five senses and stay present in the moment with them.

Do this five times, then have them share what their senses are telling them about the present moment. If you're doing this together, you can share what your senses are telling you.

End with a moment of gratitude for all our senses and the experiences they give us every day.

MANTRAS FOR BEING PRESENT

+ *My body and mind are present in the moment.*
+ *I am here right now.*
+ *I am grateful for this moment.*
+ *This moment is a miracle.*
+ *Presence is a gift that I give myself daily.*

Stress Management

Overall, stress gets a bad rap. Every time we talk about stress. or hear that someone is stressed, we assume it's a bad thing. But it's important to recognize that not all stress is bad stress. In fact, we need a healthy amount of it in our lives to function.

The important thing to remember is that some stress is healthy, but too much is not. Although it may not be pleasant at times, healthy stress can be useful. It can give you information about your surroundings, kick off a change in your life, help you meet your basic needs, and nudge you in the direction of growth. Even the excitement and slight worry or fear you may have experienced when you found out you were going to be a parent for the first time was technically stress, but that doesn't mean it was bad.

The issue arises when we are no longer experiencing the healthy type of stress or when we experience consistent prolonged periods of stress.

When the stress is continual and we never get a chance to pause and go back to baseline, it can have a negative impact on our overall health and well-being. Prolonged periods of stress—including worry, fear, anxiety and other negative emotions—can cause low energy, insomnia, aches and pains, clouded thinking, intense emotional highs and lows, increased risk of heart disease or alcohol and drug abuse, and a depressed immune system.

We as human beings are not designed to be under stress for prolonged periods of time, and it is essential that we take time to hit the pause button, give our stressed minds, bodies, and hearts some time to relax and unwind. It is also important that we model healthy stress management for our children as they learn how to navigate this increasingly challenging world.

This is where meditation comes into play.

Taking a few minutes each day to meditate can help you reduce your stress, and it can actually begin to rewire the stress center of your brain (amygdala) to start having smaller neurological and physiological reactions to stressors.

If we live in a constant state of go, go, go, do more, be more, achieve more, and we never take time to pause, it's nearly impossible for us to show up as our best selves for our families and for ourselves. The following practices are designed to help with that. Use them to hit the pause button and to model healthy stress management for your children when there is stress in your life or in your family.

Meditation Practices for Stress Management

For Adults

Note: If you'd like, you can take this meditation outside, or you can stick to indoors and use your imagination.

Begin your meditation by giving yourself permission to take a break from your stress and be present for the next few minutes.

Take three deep, cleansing breaths by breathing in through the nose and exhaling through your mouth.

Repeat the following phrase to yourself three times: *I release my stress and welcome in calm.*

Begin practicing the Relaxation Breath (page 32). Do this until you feel your body and mind begin to relax (a minute or two).

Imagine you are sitting on a chair in your favorite place to relax outdoors. Listen to the sounds around you, hear the breeze move through the trees, and smell the fresh air.

Feel the warm, comforting sunshine melt away all your stress and worry.

Stay with this image, practicing Relaxation Breath, for as long as you would like, allowing more stress to leave your body with each exhale.

For Kids + Teens

Begin your meditation by naming what you're feeling and what is causing you to feel stress or worry.

Notice where in your body you are experiencing this stress; how does it feel?

Being practicing Relaxation Breath (page 32).

On every exhale, let a small amount of your stress be released.

Continue to breathe and imagine that you are walking down a staircase. With every breath out, you take a step down the staircase and closer to relaxation.

Practice continues on next page

CH 3 Meditation Practices for the Whole Family   39

Do ten of these long breaths, and on the final exhale allow the last bit of stress to be released from your body when you reach the bottom of the staircase.

Close the meditation by repeating the following phrase to yourself three times: *I welcome relaxation into my day.*

For Little Ones

Have your child begin by naming what they are feeling, talk to them about the stress they are experiencing, and encourage them to share.

Ask them where they are feeling this stress in their body.

Have your little one begin to breathe down deep into their belly, almost like they are trying to fill a balloon.

Introduce Relaxation Breath (page 32).

Ask your child to stay with this breath and imagine that when they exhale they are blowing up a balloon and sending all of their stress into it.

Do this breath five more times, and each time they exhale encourage them to remove the stress from their body into the balloon.

After the final breath, ask them to stay still just for a moment to enjoy a quiet moment of relaxation for their bodies and minds. If they like, they can mentally "pop" the balloon filled with stress.

MANTRAS FOR STRESS MANAGEMENT

+ *(inhale) Peace. (exhale) Stress.*

+ *I am at peace in this moment.*

+ *Relaxation comes to me with ease.*

+ *I release all stress from my body and mind.*

+ *Each breath I take fills my body with relaxation and calm.*

Anxiety

Anxiety is something that can plague us at every age and stage of life. According to the Anxiety and Depression Association of America (ADAA), anxiety disorders are the most common mental illness in the United States, affecting over 40 million adults over the age of eighteen. The statistics for kids and teens are even more shocking: The ADAA reports that roughly 31 percent of teens, ages thirteen to eighteen, have an anxiety disorder, as do nearly 6 million children over the age of three.

Anxiety is something that most of us have likely experienced at one point or another, but, unlike stress—which, again, can be healthy in certain situations—anxiety is not necessarily something we have to live with. One of the most requested meditation topics on my podcasts *Mindful in Minutes* and *Meditation Mama* are about anxiety, and though I release more episodes on this than any other topic, the requests keep coming. And honestly, I am happy about that. Because while the statistics demonstrating the rise of anxiety in our society are staggering, meditation has been scientifically proven to not only alleviate symptoms but rewire the brain to have smaller physiological anxiety responses to triggers.

When Porkchop was just born, I leaned on my meditation practice for anxiety support. Once we left the hospital, I found myself in the thick of postpartum anxiety. Specifically, it manifested into a deep fear of sleeping. I was afraid to sleep when he was sleeping in case I slept through something bad happening to him. I would keep myself up at night listening to the sound of him breathing, just so I knew he was okay. If I found myself dozing off, I would wake up in such a state of panic I could hardly handle it. So I fell back on what I knew, and that was meditation. It was my saving grace during this time (as well as talking to a trained postpartum therapist). During meditation, I sat with my feelings of anxiety, connected with my breath, and incorporated the tools I had from my meditation practice in those moments of intense fear and panic. Eventually, I was able to quell my intense fear about sleeping and, slowly, begin to get my life back.

Meditation can be a wonderful tool to help with your anxiety. But if you find your symptoms are interfering with your everyday life, a licensed and trained professional can support you. Asking for help is not weakness. Working with a trained professional and using meditation can be a wonderful combination for your mental well-being and anxiety relief.

It has been shown that any style of meditation will work to change your brain's response to anxiety triggers. So when you or a family member are experiencing deep feelings of anxiety, try these meditation practices to help return to a state of calm.

Meditation Practices for Anxiety

For Adults

Come to a comfortable position and, if you'd like, close your eyes.

Connect with your breath: How are you breathing right now?

Start slowing your breath and send it down into your belly.

Begin your Box Breath (page 32) and repeat it seven times.

Let your breath return to a natural pattern, and focus on the rise and fall of the belly as you breathe in and out effortlessly.

In your mind's eye, imagine that you are turning inward and retreating to a safe space within yourself. This space can look however you want it to, but the important thing is that it's a space where you feel safe.

Visualize what this safe space looks like and let yourself begin to relax and release your anxiety.

Tell yourself *I am safe, I am strong, I am still.*

Continue to repeat this mantra as many times as you need until you begin to feel relief from your anxiety, and continue to breathe fully.

Stay here for at least five more minutes, or as long as you would like.

For Kids + Teens

Begin by rubbing your hands on your legs for a few seconds to wake up your senses and bring yourself into your body.

Take ten deep breaths.

Begin to level out your breath and focus on each inhale and exhale by thinking "breath in" on the inhale and "breath out" on the exhale.

Do this for one minute.

Now name one thing you hear.

Name one thing you see.

Name one thing you feel.

Name one thing you smell.

Name one thing you taste.

Repeat this three more times. Check in with what you are experiencing with each sense one at a time.

Take five more deep breaths to end your meditation practice.

For Little Ones

Begin this practice by checking in with your child and asking them to identify what they are feeling or what emotion they are experiencing right now.

Hold their hands and together take five deep breaths inhaling through the nose and sighing out through the mouth.

Demonstrate how to warm their hands by rubbing them together, and then taking their warm hands on their chest to send "peace" to their heart.

Continue to breathe with them. Have them imagine that there is a flower in their hands; inhale to smell the flower, exhale to blow the petals away.

Do this for a minute or two together and end the meditation by checking in with your child again to see if they are feeling better.

MANTRAS FOR ANXIETY

+ *(inhale) Serenity. (exhale) Anxiety. I release all anxiety from my body and mind.*

+ *I am safe.*

+ *Today I live without anxiety.*

+ *This moment will pass. Just breathe and be.*

Insomnia

Okay, first things first. No matter how old your children are, or where you are in your parenting journey, chances are you are losing sleep or you have recently lost sleep because of your kids. I vividly remember one day when Porkchop was about three months old, my husband was working long shifts in the intensive care unit, and my little guy was up nearly six times a night, day in and day out. I was exhausted. No, I was destroyed. I was so tired it hurt. I couldn't think straight, and I fell to my knees in tears crying and praying to anyone who would listen to please let my baby sleep longer than forty-five minutes and help me get some rest. Months of sleep deprivation was breaking me down.

Thankfully, shortly after this plea to the universe for help, Porkchop did start sleeping more, which meant I was sleeping more. But I never fully returned to the length or quality of sleep that I once had before I was a mother. Sure, my child was sleeping more, but my sleep was still fragmented. My mind was busy, and I wasn't getting the sleep that I needed to function during the day.

One thing I learned during this time was that sleep deprivation is not a badge of honor. Getting less sleep didn't make me a better mom. Constantly worrying about every little thing didn't mean I loved my child more than other parents. It just meant I was getting less sleep, and was struggling to show up as my best self because of it.

Living in a constant state of sleep deprivation can wreak havoc on your body, mind, and soul. Waking up in the middle of the night to a racing mind or constant worry will wear you down. It also, frankly, solves nothing and only make things worse.

We as adults are not the only ones who struggle with sleep. Children can struggle with insomnia for a plethora of reasons. They could be going through a neurological leap, having separation anxiety, waking up and then struggling to fall asleep again, or maybe having nightmares (see page 134 for meditations on nightmares).

The thing about insomnia is that it's not an overnight fix. You have to start simple. Prioritizing your sleep is a wonderful way to take care of yourself and model self-care for your children.

If you or your children are struggling to fall asleep or stay asleep at night, try these evening meditation practices to quiet your mind before bed and lull you to sleep. If your insomnia is getting to the point where meditation is not helping, and lack of sleep is interfering with your everyday life, consider talking with a doctor.

Meditation Practices for Insomnia

For Adults

Get comfortable in your bed, and settle in. Get as cozy and as comfortable as possible. Turn off distractions.

Give yourself permission to set your worries aside for the next ten minutes and give your body time to rest and relax.

Tune in to your breath, and let it slow down naturally.

Begin a body scan by starting with your toes.

Spend one breath cycle on each one of your toes, allow them to "fall asleep" after your exhale. Repeat this process as you move your attention upward through different parts of your body. As you inhale, focus your attention on a new body part. As you exhale, that body parts goes to sleep.

Slowly move through every part of your body, ending with the crown of your head.

When you have scanned through your body, continue to breathe into the belly, and feel yourself relax by 1 percent with each breath out, moving closer and closer to sleep with each cycle until you eventually drift off.

For Kids + Teens

Get comfortable. Turn off the lights and all distractions—including your phone—and get into bed.

Tell yourself three times: *Now is the time for sleep.*

Feel where your body meets your bed; notice these areas and let your body melt and relax into your bed.

Start breathing into your belly, taking full inhales and exhales.

Let your breath slow down, and lengthen your exhales a little more than your inhales.

On your next inhale, think *inhale, 1,* then when you exhale think *exhale, 2.*

Continue to count your inhales and exhales with a number until you reach 50.

If you lose your place when counting, just start again at 1 and count your breaths until you reach 50.

When you reach the end, count down from 50 and back to one.

For Little Ones

Have your child get into bed and get comfortable.

If they are worried or anxious, remind them that they are safe in their room.

Begin to breathe together, guiding them to move the breath down low into the belly.

Now have your child close their eyes and imagine a balloon in their mind (ask them what color it is).

Have your child inhale for a count of 4, instructing them that they are "preparing to blow up the balloon."

Then, have them exhale for a count of 7, instructing them to imagine that they are "filling up the balloon."

Continue with this balloon imagery. Tell them that as the balloon get bigger and bigger, they will get sleepier and sleepier. Continue until they fall asleep.

MANTRAS FOR INSOMNIA

+ *I give myself permission to rest.*
+ *Sleep comes to me when I need it.*
+ *I become more relaxed with each breath.*
+ *I go to sleep with ease and get the rest I need.*
+ *Each night is a good night of sleep.*

Frustration

I am going to be honest here. I don't think I ever fully understood what frustration was until I had a toddler. If you've ever had a child between the ages of 1½ to 3, you know exactly what I am talking about and the level of frustration that your once sweet little baby, now wolverine demon on a triple espresso, can bring out of you.

I remember vividly one of those days, the first of many where all that could go wrong went wrong. Porkchop was just off, and this made him emotional. He wasn't talking yet and was frustrated at many things, so he started expressing his frustration by hitting. No one was safe; he would get frustrated and turn and hit whatever was closest to him. It could be me, the dog, the refrigerator, his favorite stuffed animal baby beluga, or even his own head.

Again, another honest moment. This horrified me. I hated the hitting. It made me second-guess everything I was doing as a parent, and it filled me with frustration and shame that my child was hitting others. What had I possibly done wrong to have him start this behavior?

It got to the point where the hitting and the general fussing and neediness of a toddler brought my frustration to a level where I felt like I was living in a pressure cooker. This particular day, I hit my breaking point. Porkchop for the one millionth time splashed his hand in the dog's water bowl and tipped it over. I took the bowl and put it up on the counter. So he screamed, walked right up to me, and smacked me in the face. It wasn't the first time he hit me, and it wouldn't be the last, but there was something that time that made me snap. I cried, which made him cry, and then he hit me again, and I felt all my frustration pour out of me like a crack in a dam that couldn't hold the pressure anymore and just burst right open.

And there we were. Two extremely frustrated people, upset, angry, and unable to fully communicate with one another. And so we both just cried. It wasn't pretty, it isn't a moment I'm proud of, but I remember thinking *ah, this is what true frustration looks like.*

And after a few minutes of crying, Porkchop and I took some deep breaths, and we held each other. I looked into his big, blue, teary eyes and I saw the same frustration I was feeling mirrored in his own eyes. And I got it. He was frustrated. He was feeling what I felt, but he just didn't know what to do with these feelings. So he hit. He lashed out with his hands.

I learned a lot in that moment.

I recognized that no matter how big or small we are, sometimes things are frustrating, extremely frustrating.

Upon reflection I came to realize that being frustrated didn't mean I was a bad mom, or that somehow if Porkchop frustrated me that meant I didn't love him, but it did mean that I needed to start recognizing the cracks in the dam before it became a full-blown flood.

Two things could exist. I could love Porkchop with every cell of my being, and I could get very frustrated with being punched in the face by an emotional toddler. Frustration is a natural emotion that will pop up in your life and your children's lives. The following meditations are designed to help you release some frustration when it is running hot.

Meditation Practices for Frustration

For Adults

Begin your meditation by getting comfortable and allowing yourself to notice and feel your frustration without judgment.

Feel yourself turn inward toward a space of quiet and stillness.

Slow down your breath, and allow your awareness to fall on the wave of breath moving in and out of you.

Mentally scan your body and notice where you are experiencing frustration and what it feels like.

Visualize these areas of frustration as if they are made of concrete: hard, heavy, and rigid on your body.

As you continue to breathe, notice the concrete begin to crumble, break apart, and fall off your body.

Continue to breathe and let the frustration crumble away as it is released.

Visualize crystal-clear water coming and washing your body clean from all residues of the concrete and with it the frustration.

Close your practice by taking three deep cleansing breaths, enjoying the lightness of the body now that you have released your frustration.

For Kids + Teens

Get comfortable and, if you'd like, close your eyes. Take three deep breaths to settle in.

Begin your meditation by naming what emotions you are feeling in your heart and body right now.

Connect with your breath and start breathing down low into your belly, slowing down the breath.

Visualize a light starting at the top of your head like the laser of a scanner and watch it move from the top of your body to the bottom, noticing all the parts of your body that are feeling frustrated or angry.

Continue to breathe, and as you inhale imagine peace and happiness coming into your body. When you exhale, imagine that all your frustration and anger are leaving your body.

Do this as many times as you need to until you feel your frustration leaving your body.

End your meditation with three deep breaths, and give yourself a hug if it feels good.

For Little Ones

In moments of frustration, have your child first state out loud that they are frustrated, to make sure they understand what they're feeling.

Guide them through a Relaxation Breath where their exhales are longer than their inhales.

Remind them it's okay to feel frustrated but that this breath can help them relax when they feel this way.

Have your child take a deep breath in while counting on the fingers of one hand, 1, 2, 3, 4, 5. On the exhale, put the fingers back down, one at a time, 1, 2, 3, 4, 5.

Have them do this five times or until their frustration starts to feel better.

MANTRAS FOR FRUSTRATION

+ *(inhale) Patience. (exhale) Frustration.
  I release frustration from my body and heart.*

+ *With each exhale, I release frustration.*

+ *In moments of frustration, I return to
  my breath.*

+ *I step back, take a breath, and know this
  will pass.*

Gratitude

Gratitude is something we talk about when we teach our children how to say thank you. But how often do you move past just talking about gratitude and truly embody the practice? Not only is gratitude a lovely thing to practice and teach your children about, but it is something that has been shown to truly change our lives. In the section on Joy (page 55), you learn that doing several small things each day to boost our happiness is the best way to overcome pessimism. One of the best ways to incorporate these little mood-boosting moments throughout your day is by practicing gratitude. In fact, studies have shown that a regular gratitude practice can increase your optimism by 10 percent, your sleep quality by 25 percent, and your overall well-being by 10 percent.

When I think about gratitude, I think about life itself. I think about every single breath that I haven't been guaranteed, every moment that I get to live, breathe, and be, and how miraculous it is that I am here, right now. There is something to be grateful for every moment of every day, even when life feels like it is falling apart, because those moments, too, are miraculous.

To be alive is a miracle. Each day we get to learn lessons, we get to feel, we get to be present on earth for all of this. Even on those days when we feel that there is nothing to be grateful for, we can still be grateful that we are here, feet planted on earth. We have been given another breath and another moment to experience life.

What better way to show gratitude for the life we have been given than to really live our lives and be present for each moment? If you want to explore gratitude within yourself or with your family, give these meditations a try.

Meditation Practices for Gratitude

For Adults

Start your meditation by getting comfortable, closing your eyes, and igniting the feeling of gratitude deep in your heart.

If you're struggling to find that feeling, think about a person, a pet, or something in your life that you are always grateful for.

Visualize gratitude in your mind. What color is it? What does it feel like? Does it have a texture? This will be different for everyone.

Allow your heart to be filled with the feeling and image of gratitude.

With each breath in and each breath out, allow the feeling of gratitude to grow bigger and go beyond your heart, until it has spread out into every cell of your body and begins to radiate out of you.

Stay with this feeling of gratitude until you feel your meditation is complete.

For Kids + Teens

Begin by coming to a comfortable position, close your eyes, and welcome gratitude into your heart by thinking of someone you love.

Begin to focus on your breath.

As you inhale think, "I am grateful for . . ." , and as you exhale, name something you are grateful for.

Repeat this ten times to close your meditation.

For Little Ones

Take your child outside or go somewhere with stones on the ground (or pick up some stones before you do this and bring them home to your child).

Go outside and take a moment of gratitude for the earth and sky around you.

Start walking with your child. Ask them to pick up their favorite stones from the ground as they walk, and each time they pick one up, name something they are grateful for.

Every time they pick up a stone and name what they are grateful for, put it in a bowl or bucket.

Do this until the stones are gone or the bucket is too heavy to pick up.

Once you're done, talk about how the bucket is so heavy, because there are so many things in their life to be grateful for.

MANTRAS FOR GRATITUDE

+ *I am filled with gratitude.*

+ *I find gratitude for the small things in life.*

+ *Life is filled with beautiful moments.*

+ *I count my blessings every day.*

+ *I am grateful for another day of life.*

Finding Joy

I'm going to start this section with an uncomfortable truth: Human beings are, unfortunately, wired to have a negativity bias. This means we're not only predisposed to look at the glass as half empty but we hold on to negative experiences for longer than positive ones. This negativity bias means that a negative moment is going to hit harder and stick around longer than an equally positive moment.

If you think back to the stone age, we were designed to always be on the lookout for danger, to search for ways to keep ourselves safe, and to replay dangerous situations over and over again in our heads to figure out what went wrong and how it could go better next time. Those of us who embraced this negativity bias and ruminated on the dangerous or unpleasant parts of life lived longer because they were able to adapt and keep themselves safe in dangerous or uncomfortable situations.

Now fast forward to modern day. We are still equipped with our negativity bias, designed for our survival. However, instead of dwelling on where we last saw a bear, we now replay that one negative comment someone said to us the other day or the weird look someone gave us. We are wired to constantly look for the lesson in these tough situations in the hopes that we can avoid the negative experience again. This leads us to ruminate on the challenges, struggles, and tough times, pushing us into a deeper state of negativity.

Right about now you're probably wondering, why I would talk about negativity so much in a section that is about joy? Well, there are two main reasons. First, it is my belief that without the lows of life it is nearly impossible to enjoy the highs. Second, I believe that by changing how we look at negativity, we can reverse the way we engage with our negativity bias, ultimately helping us to better access our joy.

Studies have found that finding joy is less about doing big happy things every once in a while and more about finding small moments throughout the day to experience joy. Taking little joy breaks throughout the day is far more effective at impacting our ability to be optimistic and unlock joy than taking a vacation twice a year. These breaks could be anything that makes you smile and brings you happiness. You could try taking a few deep breaths, watching a video that always makes you laugh, putting your phone down and enjoying a hug from your kids, or doing a mini meditation break like the ones outlined below.

If you think of your happiness as a plant and your joy as the rain, it's easy to recognize that you can't thrive on just one big shower every once in a while. We need periodic watering and a regular flow of happiness into our lives to truly thrive and find joy where we are. To "water" the joy in the lives of your family members, try these mediation practices.

Meditation Practices for Finding Joy

For Adults

Begin by coming to a comfortable meditation position, and let your awareness fall on your breath.

Follow the breath as it moves effortlessly in and out of your body.

Breathe for several minutes. (*inhale*) Happiness. (*exhale*) Negativity.

In your mind's eye, imagine you are like a magnet for joy, so much happiness and joy is being drawn towards you as you breathe in.

Joy is rushing to you, filling you up and moving into every part of your life.

Welcome this joy into your heart fully, and let it pour into you.

Stay with this sensation of joy for at least five minutes.

Close your meditation by stating one thing that brings you joy.

For Kids + Teens

Take a moment to settle into a comfortable position and give yourself permission to experience joy in your life today.

Check in with how you're feeling right now and label (in your head) the emotions you're experiencing (e.g., impatient, frustrated).

Visualize a white light shining down on your head clearing away any negativity, sadness, or anything else getting in the way of your joy.

Once these negative feelings have been cleared away, imagine a golden light of joy sparking in your heart.

Let this golden light grow stronger until it is shining in every part of you, filling you with an abundance of joy.

End your practice by telling yourself three times: I am joyful and my heart is happy.

For Little Ones

Start by talking to your child about happiness and joy and what that means to each of you.

Sit together and take three deep breaths.

Have your child imagine they are a tiny sunflower in the ground.

Have them visualize a bright sun shining down on them releasing any sadness or negativity.

As the sun shines down on them, with each breath their happiness grows and they as a sunflower grow bigger too, reaching further and further up into the sky towards the joyful sun shining down on them.

Do this for a minute or so.

MANTRAS FOR JOY

+ *I welcome joy into my life.*
+ *My day is filled with small, joyful moments.*
+ *Each day is a joyful day.*
+ *My heart is filled with infinite happiness.*
+ *Joy comes to me with ease.*

Sadness

Being a parent isn't always joyful. Experiencing moments of sadness with your children is normal and does not make you a bad parent. All people experience sadness at times. Adults experience it, kids experience it, babies experience it. Sadness is a part of life, and although we are often taught to put our best foot forward, slap a smile on our face, and pretend it is all okay, the truth is sometimes it's not okay.

Life is filled with ups and downs, and you never know what is happening beneath the surface of someone's smile. When I first became a mother, I struggled with postpartum depression. I didn't even realize it at the time, because it snuck into my life in unexpected ways. Instead of crying all the time, or not being able to get out of bed, I found that I was trying to do everything all the time. I was being overly productive, trying to be a mom, run a business, have a personal life, keep my marriage together, and constantly be on the go. But what I was really doing was just trying to take my sadness and stuff it so deep down under my productivity that I couldn't see it anymore.

Stuffed down in the darkest and loneliest parts of your heart is where sadness thrives. That is where it grows, multiplies, strengthens, and takes on a life of its own. That is where it begins to take a turn for the worse, and before you know it, you're in a bad place. You don't know how you got there, but you're there, isolated, tired, and sad.

Sadness is kind of like that old piece of cheese that you have in the back of the fridge. It's been forgotten, shoved to the back to never be seen again, and in its neglected, forgotten state, it gets bigger and messier and uglier, until you finally look at it months later and it is a big, disgusting, stinky mess.

To cope with sadness, you need to bring it to light, talk about it, and have safe people to share it with. We need to have honest conversations around sadness in our lives. It is okay to be sad, and it is okay to not be okay. Without the lows of life you would never really know how incredible the highs can be. That said, we still need tools to address the lows. We need to bring sadness out from the deep, dark depths of our emotional refrigerator and call it what it is.

We will experience sadness at all points in our lives. Just this week, my son broke into tears because he was feeling sad. Then I got so tired of hearing his crying, that I started crying and then we were both crying and

sad together. After we cried, we hugged and brought our sadness into the light for one another to see. We let the light shine on our feelings, and this helped us to remember that we are never alone, even on the darkest days.

The next time sadness hits your heart or appears in your household, try these meditation practices. If you feel that your sadness is getting in the way of living your life, please also talk with someone you trust and consider seeing a licensed therapist or counselor.

Meditation Practices for Sadness

For Adults

Begin by coming to a comfortable position, giving yourself permission to feel how you are feeling and to experience sadness.

Take three deep cleansing breaths, inhaling through the nose and sighing out through the mouth.

Name how you are feeling right now, without judgment. Check in with your emotions and name what you are feeling.

When your feelings have been named, welcome in a sensation of loving kindness and compassion.

Focus on the feeling of loving kindness and compassion, and as you breathe let this feeling grow in your heart.

Visualize yourself standing in front of you and send that feeling of loving kindness and compassion to your highest self. Watch it surround yourself like a hug and help bring comfort to you and soothe your sadness.

Visualize this for as long as you would like or until you feel your sadness lifting.

For Kids + Teens

Begin your meditation practice by coming to a comfortable position, then rub your hands together until they are warm.

Once your hands are warm, place them on your heart and let the warmth sink into your heart.

Begin to breathe slowly and down into your belly.

Name how you are feeling right now.

In your heart center under your warm hands, visualize a spark of light in your heart.

This light looks like a sparkler, and it is igniting happiness into your heart and comforting you in your time of sadness.

Allow this sparkling light to move from your heart into every part of you, until your body is illuminated with joy from head to toe.

Tell yourself three times: *I release my sadness and find moments of joy in my life.*

End your meditation with three deep cleansing breaths and, if you'd like, hug yourself.

For Little Ones

Have your child begin by naming how they are feeling and why. For example: I am sad that mom has to go to work and can't stay to play with me today.

Have them close their eyes, give themselves a hug, and send love and comfort to themselves.

Have them visualize comfort and love surrounding them to soothe their sadness.

If you have a child who likes art, try having them draw what their sadness feels like and also what their comfort feels like so they can better visualize them in their mind's eye.

Encourage them to share how this practice made them feel.

MANTRAS FOR SADNESS

+ *(inhale) Joy. (exhale) Sadness.*
+ *I allow my heart to feel what it feels.*
+ *Happiness flows into my heart.*
+ *Today I feel sad, and that's okay.*
+ *My heart is happy, and my mind is clear.*

Forgiveness

Forgiveness is something I think about often. I talk with Porkchop about forgiveness, how important it is, and how good it feels. I also encourage my students to explore forgiveness in their meditation practice. Still, sometimes in my own life I struggle to let things go. Even as a meditation teacher, I can hold one heck of a grudge.

Much like our brains have learned to keep us safe from physical harm by searching for the threat in a situation, they try to keep us safe from emotional harm by remembering hurtful things people did to us so we can avoid that hurt and pain in the future. We are designed to survive and keep ourselves safe in body, mind, and heart. Holding grudges, or cultivating an unwillingness to forgive, is another way of protecting ourselves. We throw up the walls and lock the gates to keep ourselves safe from harm.

The first profound shift I had around forgiveness was during a yoga teacher training in Bali. I was finishing up the morning's practice and I was laying in savasana, meditating, like I did every morning. Nothing particularly was going on when suddenly I felt this weight lift from my chest. It was like my eyes had been opened and I realized that some of the worst things that had ever happened in my life had happened for a reason. Suddenly I understood: *It was time to give them their weight back.* I saw myself taking these heavy rocks and handing them back to people who had caused me harm, handing back the weight that I had been carrying on their behalf.

In that moment, I realized forgiveness wasn't for them but for me. The people who I chose to forgive right there in that yoga shala probably hadn't thought about me in years or wouldn't know or even care that I decided to forgive them. They may not have realized that I was holding on to anything they had done. But that didn't matter. In giving them their weight back, I was choosing to release the pain, hurt, and weight that I had been dragging around for years. It was finally time.

To forgive is to create freedom in your heart and to choose to drop that weight—even if the one you need to forgive is yourself. The next time you find yourself struggling to forgive, ask yourself, am I ready to drop this weight? Or do I want to carry it around for a while longer? The choice is always yours, and you can choose when, if ever, you release that weight. But remember, it becomes awfully hard to fly if you're weighed down. If you feel ready to release that weight, or you are working on forgiveness as a family, try these meditation practices.

Meditation Practices for Forgiveness

For Adults

Take a moment to get comfortable in your meditation position and give yourself permission to feel however you are feeling.

Set the intention of forgiveness for your practice and visualize what you are ready to forgive as a heavy weight being carried on your shoulders.

Connect with your breath and send it low into the belly.

Ignite the feeling of forgiveness within your heart, think about how it feels to be forgiven and what forgiveness feels like for you.

Let this feeling grow from your heart until it is radiating out of your body and filling up the space around you. Give this feeling a color and see this color surround you.

Visualize the person you are forgiving standing in front of you. Look them in the eye and say *I forgive you* and imagine yourself dropping that weight.

Radiate the color of forgiveness from your heart center to their heart center and genuinely forgive and wish them well.

Continue to send this light to them for as long as you need until you know you have truly forgiven them.

For Kids + Teens

Take a moment to get comfortable. Close your eyes if it feels good and take three deep breaths.

Think about the person you want to forgive and picture them in your mind

Visualize the heaviness and weight of what you're holding onto like a block of concrete on your chest.

As you breathe, see a small seed of forgiveness in your heart and watch it begin to grow from your heart, out of your chest and eventually breaking through the concrete.

Practice continues on next page

As the seed grows and turns into a flower of forgiveness, see the concrete crumble and release from your chest.

Continue to breathe, and on the inhale, bring forgiveness into your heart by saying "I forgive myself." On the exhale, send that forgiveness to that individual by saying "I forgive you."

Do this for at least five minutes.

For Little Ones

Take a moment to talk to your child about forgiveness, who they want to forgive, and why.

Have your child put their hands on their heart and talk about what it feels like when someone forgives them.

Now ask them what color forgiveness is (if they like, they can draw a picture of forgiveness using this color).

As them to take three deep breaths while imagining sending that color of forgiveness from their heart to the heart of the person they are forgiving.

Have them send forgiveness for a minute or so.

Then ask your child how forgiveness feels and why.

MANTRAS FOR FORGIVENESS

+ *Forgiveness comes easily to me.*
+ *I forgive myself for mistakes I've made.*
+ *I release resentment and choose to forgive.*
+ *I forgive those who have caused me harm.*
+ *I am surrounded by forgiveness.*

Letting Go

One of my favorite Rumi quotes is "Try something different. Surrender."

When I think about surrender and letting go, I think about the ocean. I think about the tides, the waves, the depth of the salty water and how you have two options if you want to move through that water. You can fight it, trying to move through the water by force, or you can surrender and go with the tide. Life can feel like you're swimming upstream, fighting the tide, and struggling vainly to try to get where you "think" you ought to go but all the while staying in the same spot.

For me, swimming against the tide and fighting the waves meant trying to force myself to look a certain way, be a certain way, have things happen at "the right time," and basically do everything I could to maintain control over every small detail of my life. But I was stuck, swimming endlessly against waves that kept me stagnant regardless of my effort.

So I tried something new. I surrendered. I told myself, *let it be easy. Let it happen how it is meant to happen.* For me, trust and surrender often go hand in hand. To fully surrender, you need to trust that everything will happen how it's supposed to and that life isn't happening *to* you but happening *for* you.

There will be times when its necessary to fight the current, and the beautiful but challenging thing is that you have to choose those moments for yourself. Using a meditation practice, like those that follow, to connect with your true self and decide when it's time to fight and when it's time to surrender, can be a simple but profound practice. I encourage you to try, it may show you how many unnecessary waves you swim against each day.

Meditation Practices for Letting Go

For Adults

Begin your meditation by coming to a comfortable position, closing your eyes, and accepting what you are feeling right now.

Name what it is that you would like to let go of.

Follow your breath as it dances in and out of your body.

Tune in to your body, notice where you are physically holding this thing.

Practice continues on next page

As you continue to breathe, feel that part of your body begin to soften and release.

With each breath, feel your grasp on that thing soften a bit more.

Complete your meditation by stating three times, I release _____ from my body, mind, and heart.

For Kids + Teens

Begin your meditation by thinking about what you're ready to let go of.

Think of this thing, and hold it clearly in your mind.

Now imagine that thing is like a string that is attached to your body.

Take three deep breaths, and after the third breath imagine using a pair of large gold scissors to cut the string and release what you were holding onto.

Once this thing has been removed, tell yourself *I allow myself to move with the flow of life.*

For Little Ones

Have your child name the things they are ready to let go of.

While your child sits or relaxes in their meditation, have them visualize one thing they are ready to let go of as a balloon.

As they breathe, they imagine each exhale filling up the balloon.

When the balloon is full of breath, ask them to say good-bye and to imagine letting go of the balloon. Wave as it floats away!

MANTRAS FOR LETTING GO

+ *(inhale) New beginnings. (exhale) The past.*
+ *I release all that no longer serves me.*
+ *I choose to let go of what has been bothering me.*
+ *I flow with the tide of life.*
+ *Letting go is essential to my health.*

Trust

When I think about trust, I think about breath. All day long, we breathe in and out, not really thinking about it and just trusting that every time we exhale, another inhale will follow. If we didn't trust that this process would work, we would go into a total panic in between each breath. We most likely wouldn't sleep at night, because what if we forgot to breathe and died?

I don't use this example to give anyone anxiety or to make them worry about going to sleep at night. I use it because it shows us that we are designed to trust. There are so many things that we must choose whether or not to trust: our intuition, people, situations, politicians, pretty much anyone and anything we encounter in any given day. Some things are easier to trust, like our breath, while others, like certain people or our own intuition, can be more challenging. Depending on our circumstances or the way we grew up, trust can be a difficult concept to embrace. But I would like to boldly suggest that one thing you can always trust is your gut. Your own internal guide will keep you on your path.

Trust is in everything that we do. We have to trust that we did our best to raise our children and prepare them for the real world outside of the walls of our home. We have to trust that we are making the best decisions for ourselves and our families. And we have to trust our own intuition even if it doesn't make sense at the time.

To trust is to surrender to the idea that we don't always need to have the answers or see the results immediately. Trust is a deep knowing that our internal guide will help us in times of need and that we will do the best we can with what we have.

If you are someone who loves control—and, let's be real, who doesn't love control?—working on growing your trust can help you loosen the reins a bit and soften the grip that you have (or want) on life. If this sounds intriguing or inspiring, the following meditations are for you!

Meditation Practices for Trust

For Adults

Come to a comfortable position, and begin to take slow, smooth, steady breaths.

Follow your breath, and notice how the air feels cool as it enters your body and warm as it leaves your body.

Pay attention to this for several minutes.

Notice the small moments in between each breath when you are completely full of air before the exhale and completely empty of air before the next inhale.

Each time you are in one of the moments in between breath, repeat the phrase, *I trust.*

Repeat this for at least five minutes, focusing on the trust you place in your own breath.

For Kids + Teens

Find a quiet place to meditate for a few minutes where you will be comfortable and undisturbed.

Begin to practice a balancing breath.

Visualize a red light growing down from your tailbone into the earth, grounding you and filling you with a sense of calm.

Now visualize a white light shining up toward the sky from the crown of your head, connecting you with the universe.

Allow yourself to feel the connection between the earth, yourself, and the universe and know that all will be okay.

Close your meditation by telling yourself three times: *I trust the process, and I know the universe will take care of me.*

For Little Ones

Before starting the practice, gather some blocks or something your child can stack.

Begin the practice by having them come to a quiet place and visualize what trust feels like and looks like.

As they think about trust, have them name things that can build trust, for example, "Mommy always comes to pick me up from school" or "My sister always holds my hand when we cross the street." Add a block for everything they name. This is their "trust tower."

Then have them name things that can break down trust, such as, lying or stealing something that doesn't belong to you. Remove a block for everything that they name.

Talk about how they can build a trust tower with others through their actions, and how they should expect a trust tower from others, too.

MANTRAS FOR TRUST

+ *(inhale) Trust. (exhale) Doubt.*

+ *I am filled with unconditional trust.*

+ *I know there is a plan for me.*

+ *Trusting comes easily to me.*

+ *I trust the process of life.*

Self-Confidence

Many of us, especially women, develop habits early in life of questioning ourselves, making ourselves small and agreeable, and comparing ourselves to others. We measure ourselves against others, whether it's against the other students in class or the other parents coaching the soccer team. We may even compare our children to other children. These comparisons can be a sledgehammer to our confidence because there will always be someone better than you—just as there will always be someone worse than you. This constant need to be "good" or looking outward for external validation can give a microphone to the internal voice that says we aren't good enough or that we shouldn't be confident in who we are.

It's heartbreaking how many people—and especially how many children—lack self-confidence and are afraid to step into their light. Each of us is one of a kind. We are given a soul that belongs only to us, and we have a unique light to share with the world. When we hide it away, everything becomes dark.

The funny thing about confidence is that we are often taught that to be confident is to be arrogant or to lead with our ego. Truly, confidence is just trusting in your unique abilities and allowing your light to shine and illuminate the space around you.

Your bright light does not dim another's. In fact, it gives those around you permission to shine their light too.

As you explore self-confidence both personally and with your children, consider how you may be hiding your light and staying in the darkness of negative self-talk, self-doubt, and low self-esteem. Try these meditation practices when you need a little extra spark to light up your confidence.

Meditation Practices for Self-Confidence

For Adults

Get comfortable, close your eyes, and tune in to your body and breath.

Connect with the feeling of confidence. Perhaps recall a memory of a time when you felt confident.

Embody this feeling, as you visualize a bright yellow light sparking in your abdomen and shining in all directions.

Continue to breathe. Notice how each breath causes the light to grow, like adding oxygen to a burning flame.

As you breathe, the light continues to grow and illuminate the space all around you, and your feelings of self-confidence grow.

Continue to breathe and grow your light. Tell yourself three times:
I allow my light to shine, I am confident in who I am.

Stay here for five minutes, basking in your light and your newly boosted confidence.

For Kids + Teens

Prepare for your meditation by finding a comfortable position with your back tall, and take three deep breaths.

Begin to practice begin to practice the 3-count breath, which is based on the 3-count breath.

Inhale in thirds: with each short inhale, imagine you are pulling a burst of confidence into your body, until your lungs are completely full of air and your mind full of confidence. On the long exhale, release all self-doubt, negative self-talk, and fear in one big gust of air.

Continue to breathe this way ten times.

Then yourself three times: *I am filled with confidence.*

For Little Ones

Repeating mantras and affirmations is a great way to help your children boost their confidence.

Have your child take three deep breaths and then repeat each of the following mantras three times—or until you can see their confidence:

- I can do hard things.
- I believe in myself.
- I am awesome.
- I do good things and I try hard.

MANTRAS FOR SELF-CONFIDENCE

+ *(inhale) Confidence. (exhale) Self-doubt.*
+ *Self-confidence comes to me with ease.*
+ *I allow my light to shine in all situations.*
+ *I am secure in who I am and what I do.*
+ *I am confident in my abilities.*

Worthiness

Before we dive into this topic, let's clear something up: You've been lied to.

Every reason that you feel like you aren't good enough or aren't worthy of the good and wonderful things in this world—they're all lies. You know the ones I'm talking about. That little voice in the back of your head that says you aren't doing enough, or you aren't worthy enough, or that you aren't a good enough parent, or that if you just achieved this one milestone then you would be enough. Those are all lies.

We are programmed to believe this false narrative that no matter how you arrange the pieces of your life, they never quite add up. This simply isn't true.

Think about the first time you held your child. Did you hold them and look down into their sweet eyes and think, "Wow, you have a lot of work to do if you're ever going to be enough for me."? No! Absolutely not. More likely, you looked down into the eyes of your child and you thought, "You're perfect." You recognized the wholeness and worthiness of this tiny human being in your arms from the moment you laid eyes on them, and with some practice, self-acceptance, and compassion, you can recognize it in yourself, too.

I'm going to let you in on a little secret. You are already whole. You were born whole, you remain whole, and you will take your last breath on earth whole. We all come into this world a complete human being, worthy of love and respect, and capable of incredible things. But somewhere along the way we forget just how special and worthy we are.

Knowing that you are enough is not about what you own, or what you've accomplished, or what you look like. It is about looking at yourself the way you looked at your child and recognizing the beauty of your soul. It's about knowing that even though you are human and innately flawed and you will make mistakes, you are still enough, right here and right now. Worthiness doesn't ask us to be perfect; in fact it asks us to recognize that we will never be perfect and that is okay. No matter what, you are and always will be worthy and whole. You don't need to prove this to anyone else because no one else can affirm your worth. That is something that you and only you can do, and I assure you, you *can* do it.

If you or one of your children need a reminder of your worth, use these practices and mantras to cultivate a sense of wholeness within.

Meditation Practices for Worthiness

For Adults

Take a moment to clear your mind and release expectations.

Bring your awareness to the breath. Stay with your breath until your mind begins to quiet.

In your mind's eye, see yourself standing in front of you. Look yourself in the eye, as if looking into your child's eyes, and see how whole and worthy you are.

Look at yourself, and begin to repeat the following mantras on each breath:

- (*inhale*) I am enough.
- (*exhale*) I am worthy and whole.

Breathe, be with yourself, look into your eyes and see your worth.

Continue breathing while visualizing and repeating the mantra for at least five minutes, or for as long as you would like.

For Kids + Teens

Take a moment to get comfortable, close your eyes, and settle in.

Connect with your breath, slow it down, and take five deep breaths.

Soften your body by scanning from your feet, up to the top of your head, relaxing each part as you go.

Continue with deep breaths.

As you breathe, repeat the following mantras as many times as necessary for you to really feel the words and believe what you are saying:

- I appreciate who I am.
- I am worthy, I am whole.
- Making a mistake does not make me a bad person.
- I am worthy of love and respect.
- I can do hard things.
- I am exactly who I was meant to be.
- Today and every day I am enough, no matter what.

Seal your meditation by placing your hands on your heart, feeling it beating and filled with worth.

Little Ones

Grab a small puzzle or take a piece of paper and cut it into ten squares.

Sit quietly with your child for a moment with your hands on your heart and have your child do the same.

Send love from your hearts to one another.

Begin to pick up the puzzle pieces or paper squares.

On each puzzle piece or piece of paper, have your child say or write one thing that makes them unique.

Then on their own, or with your help, put the pieces of paper together, or put the puzzle together.

Show your child how all their "unique pieces" make up one whole puzzle or piece of paper, when put together. Tell them that they don't have to do anything to be whole and be themselves.

Then together repeat three times: *I am worthy, I am whole, I am enough.*

To seal the meditation, take a big breath in and a big breath out.

MANTRAS FOR WORTHINESS

+ *I am enough.*

+ *I am worthy of good things.*

+ *I am exactly who I was meant to be.*

+ *Today and every day I am enough, no matter what.*

+ *I treat myself with love and respect.*

Hyperactivity

Over twenty years ago, back when floppy disks and Blockbuster were a thing, I was a child recently diagnosed with attention deficit disorder (ADD). I was quiet, I didn't participate much in school, and I struggled with my grades. If I'm being honest, this was one of the hardest times of my childhood because I often heard that my struggles with school were because I wasn't trying hard enough or because I was just dumb.

But I wasn't dumb, I was me. And ultimately, I learned that "me" was someone with ADD. Notably, at my time of diagnosis the *H* was missing. This meant that I was diagnosed with attention deficit disorder and I didn't have the hyperactivity component. However, more than twenty years later and after much more research into the brain and hyperactivity, I realize that I do in fact have the hyperactivity, it just isn't exactly what we thought it was back then.

At the time, it was believed that hyperactivity just meant you were a busy child, usually a boy, who got in trouble and couldn't sit still and was all over the place. Common signs of hyperactivity include struggling to be still in calm or quiet surroundings, fidgeting, and excessive physical movement. However, now we know that hyperactivity can also show up as excessive talking, acting impulsively, interrupting conversations, or struggling to mentally focus on one task.

At the time, I thought the diagnosis was a bit of a death sentence. What I didn't realize then but know now was that my ADHD isn't what would hold me back but the thing that would propel me towards my success. My ability to be impulsive at times gave me just the right amount of recklessness that I needed to be bold and take the leap in business. My constant chatter set me up for a career of teaching and podcasting, and my struggle to focus on one thing at a time meant life was never boring. I was always thinking outside of the box, and my creativity would lead me to the life I have today.

Studies tell us that meditation can help thicken the prefrontal cortex, which is a part of the brain involved in focus, planning, and impulse control. It can also help to raise the dopamine level in the brain, which tends to not be as abundant in people with ADHD. Even a few minutes of meditation a day can help those of us with ADHD take our wild crazy minds from struggling to thriving. Remember, sometimes the thing that we think makes us weird might be the thing that makes us shine.

When your mind feels like it is running a mile a minute, try these short and simple meditations to help slow down the activity of the body and mind to focus on the here and now.

Meditation Practices for Hyperactivity

For Adults

Start your practice by taking three deep breaths.

Allow your awareness to fall on your belly.

Focus on the rise and fall of the belly as you breathe in and out for five minutes or until you find yourself coming back to center.

Every time your mind wanders, gently guide it back to the breath, over and over again.

When your five minutes of meditation are complete, gently return to the present moment.

For Kids + Teens

Try taking your meditation outside when you are feeling fidgety or are struggling to slow down.

Step outside and take a few deep breaths, taking in your surroundings.

Begin to walk slowly and with intention.

Focus on your feet touching the ground with each step.

Every time you get distracted, bring your awareness back to your feet touching the ground with each step.

Walk for five to ten minutes, or until you find yourself calming down.

For Little Ones

Have your child slow down their movements, or even become completely still, if they can handle stopping their bodies fully, by sitting or lying down.

Have your child take three deep breaths.

Now have them imagine that when they inhale, the breath is like a gold ribbon, and when they exhale, they are slowly breathing gold glitter out of their mouths.

Repeat this "glitter breathing" five times and then tell them they can get back up and return to what they were doing.

MANTRAS FOR HYPERACTIVITY

+ *I complete one thing at a time.*
+ *As I breathe, the exhale calms me.*
+ *I take my time and focus on one thing.*
+ *Stillness and focus come to me with ease.*
+ *My mind is still and my body is quiet.*

Concentration

One of the most talked-about benefits of meditation is its effect on concentration. No matter your age or stage of life, the ability to concentrate on one thing at a time is essential. Nothing is more challenging or frustrating than hopping around from task to task, never settling or focusing on one thing to see to completion.

Every time you practice single-pointed concentration, you increase your capacity to focus on a single task or idea for a longer time. Marathon runners don't just start out with marathons; they start with shorter runs. Likewise, give yourself time to "strengthen" your concentration muscles with regular training. Meditation is absolutely one of the best ways to do this.

These check-in meditation practices are great for when you need to quickly clear your mind and get into a focused or flow state.

Meditation Practices for Concentration

For Adults

Start your meditation practice by getting comfortable, closing your eyes, and releasing expectations.

Connect with your breath. Feel it flowing in and out of your body and beginning to slow down.

As you breathe, imagine that each breath is clearing your mind, removing distractions and chatter from your brain.

Breathe for about three minutes to clear your mind.

Begin to count your breaths, think *inhale, 1, exhale, 2.*

Take your time counting each inhale and exhale. Try to count to 100. If you lose your spot, begin again. Do this until you get to 100 without disruption.

Over time this practice will become easier, and eventually you will be able to count to 100 without starting over and may be able to count down from 100 as well. That's your concentration muscles getting stronger!

For Kids + Teens

Get comfortable, sitting tall and straight. Choose one of the mantras from the end of this section that resonates with you.

Close your eyes and take three deep breaths.

Begin to breathe slowly for one minute.

After one minute, continue to breathe. After each exhale, repeat your mantra.

Try to repeat your mantra fifteen times without getting distracted. If you lose track, that's okay; just start again at 1.

Do this until you can repeat your mantra fifteen times without getting distracted and having to start over.

For Little Ones

This meditation for the little ones replicates the exercise for adults, with a lower number of breaths. Choose a number that feels reasonable, such as fifteen or twenty. You can sit together and complete this meditation while holding hands, or just be together in quiet.

Invite your child to get comfortable and start to pay attention to their breaths.

As they breathe, ask them to imagine that each breath is clearing their mind, removing distractions and chatter.

When they are breathing calmly, invite them to start to count their breaths: *inhale, 1, exhale, 2.*

Invite them to continue breathing and counting, until they reach the number you chose for them. If they lose their spot, they can begin again at 1. Do this until they reach their number without disruption.

Over time, you can have your children increase the number of breaths they count in this exercise so that they are being challenged but can still be successful in counting without getting distracted.

MANTRAS FOR CONCENTRATION

+ *I focus on one thing at a time.*
+ *Each breath brings me clarity and concentration.*
+ *My mind is clear and focused.*
+ *I can focus when I need to.*
+ *Concentration comes easily to me.*

Fear

One of my favorite quotes of all time comes from a lovely book called *The Yamas and Niyamas* by Deborah Adele. And that quote is, "There are two types of fear. The fear that keeps you alive, and the fear that keeps you from living." The first time I read this in my 200-hour yoga teacher training, it completely changed the way that I looked at fear.

After reading that single quote, I began to realize that the point of life isn't to live without fear but to continue to live amidst the fear. Being a parent is scary; this world, if we're being completely honest, is kind of scary, and it fills me with fear. I sometimes find myself thinking about all the scary things that could happen to Porkchop, and when I go down that rabbit hole, it just becomes too much. It makes me want to pack up the whole family, move to a remote village in Iceland, and live a quiet, off-the-grid life in solitude.

But that's not realistic. Although there are some fears that are valid and keep me alive (for example, am I afraid to walk alone in bear country with an open jar of peanut butter smeared over my body? Yes!), some of my fears keep me from living. From a young age, I developed a fear of flying, and I put off taking my first family vacation after Porkchop was born, because the thought of putting my entire family on an airplane terrified me.

Fear is not innately a bad thing. It is an important physiological response that is essential to our survival. But we can't always rely solely on our physiological responses; we need to ask logic to weigh in, too.

I've often used this idea of two fears to call out my own BS. I'll ask myself, when fear creeps in, is this fear keeping me alive? Or is this fear keeping me from living? More times than not, it's keeping me from living, and I use meditation to clarify between the two.

Here are three meditation practices you can use when fears that keep you from living creep into your life and you're looking to quell them.

Meditation Practices for Fear

For Adults

Take a few minutes to step away, be alone, and meditate in a quiet place. Come to a comfortable position and settle in. It will help if you can have your feet flat on the ground for this meditation.

Take three deep breaths, filling your lungs with soothing air.

Visualize that roots are growing down from your hips, legs and feet and anchoring into the earth.

See these roots spread out deep and wide.

As you begin to follow your breath in and out in a natural rhythm, visualize your fear as red energy leaving your body through your roots as you exhale and dissipating into the earth.

On the inhale, visualize peace of mind and bravery as cool, bright blue energy that enters your body through your roots.

Repeat this visualization until you feel your fears have left you, or at least calmed down, and your heart is full of courage.

For Kids + Teens

Find a comfortable and quiet place where you can be alone for a few moments.

Focus on your breath, and let your exhales become longer than your inhales.

Ask yourself, where do I feel fear in my body?

As you continue to breathe with longer exhales, visualize a blue light shining down on the parts of your body that are experiencing fear.

Watch this blue light begin to melt away your fear.

As your fear melts under the cool blue light, continue to repeat *I am calm, I am confident, I am not afraid.*

Repeat this mantra and visualization for three minutes, or until you feel calm entering your body.

For Little Ones

If your child is having a fear response, teach them this 4-3-7 Relaxation Breath, which has been shown to quiet the fight-or-flight mechanism in the body.

Begin by taking your child onto your lap or holding them in a way that comforts them.

Hold their hands and tell them that you will breathe through the fear together.

Start doing the Relaxation Breath with them. Have your child inhale for 4, hold for 3, and exhale for 7.

Guide them through this five times or more, or until the fear has left their body.

MANTRAS FOR FEAR

+ *(inhale) Courage. (exhale) Fear.*
+ *I am not burdened by my fear.*
+ *I release the fears that keep me from living.*
+ *I am brave and face my fear.*
+ *My heart is filled with courage and strength.*

Quiet the Mind

I want you to think about something for a second. We have an average of 60,000 thoughts per day. To put it into context, there are just over 15,000 drops of water in one gallon. The number of thoughts you have in a single day is equivalent to the number of drops of water it takes to fill 4 gallons. That's a lot of thoughts! Our thoughts are like a constant drip, drip, drip of water running in the back of our minds all day long, and by the end of the day you've amassed a near flood. That is what is happening in your mind every day.

People often tell me that they "could never meditate" because their minds are "too busy." That the mind is busy is no surprise; our mind is designed that way! The misconception is that meditation is for people with a magical off switch rendering the mind completely clear and devoid of chatter. In truth, you think about a lot when you meditate. The point of meditation isn't to shut off all your thoughts but to allow your mind to return to your point of concentration again and again after those thoughts pop into your mind. Meditation is allowing the thoughts to become background noise, like the distant drip of a leaky faucet, while you focus on your point of concentration.

In those moments when you're ready to let the drip, drip, drip of the mind become background noise try these meditation practices.

Meditation Practices for Quieting the Mind

For Adults

Come to a comfortable position, close your eyes, and begin by acknowledging that it's okay to have thoughts during this practice. Choose to welcome them as they come and go.

Take a few deep, easy breaths, let your shoulders slide down your back, and your jaw relax.

Settle into an easy, effortless breath.

In your mind's eye, visualize that you are standing by a lake. The water is murky, there is silt and debris in the water.

As you continue to breathe, imagine that the silt, sand, and debris in the water slowly starts to sink to the bottom of the lake.

Practice continues on next page

After a few rounds of breath, continue to watch the water clear and become still.

Continue to visualize this process until the water of the lake is clear and like a pane of glass.

Feel your mind become quiet, still, and clear like the water of the lake.

As you breathe and become still, allow yourself to enjoy the quiet and stillness within you.

Stay with this visualization for five minutes or until you are ready to return to your day.

For Kids + Teens

Begin by taking three deep breaths, inhaling through your nose and sighing out through your mouth.

Now begin to practice a balancing breath.

Continue to breathe in this way as you visualize a storm outside. See the rain, hear the thunder, and watch the lighting flashing in the sky.

As you continue to breathe slowly (in for 4, out for 4), watch the storm begin to clear.

First the thunder and lightning stops, then the rain slows down, and then the clouds lift.

Continue to breathe until the storm has completely passed and the sun is coming out.

Imagine your thoughts are like this storm: The more you breathe, the further they drift away, until your mind is clear and happy as a sunny sky.

For Little Ones

This activity is a called a "meditation jar." You will need an empty, clear glass jar with a lid, glitter glue, and water.

Mix 1 cup of hot water with 2 tablespoons of glitter glue in an empty, clear glass jar. You can add some extra loose glitter if your child has lots of thoughts (or just loves glitter).

Screw the lid of the jar back on tight (you may want to glue it). Give the jar a shake and then let it sit until the water and glass cools down.

Invite your child to sit with you and hand them the jar.

Have the child shake the jar and show them how busy the "thoughts" (glitter) are.

Guide your child through some gentle breaths while they watch the glitter swirl and settle in the jar. Explain to them that their mind is like the jar: as they breathe, their "thoughts" settle to the bottom of the jar and the water becomes clear, like their minds.

Have them repeat this exercise, as you sit and breathe with your child until they feel like their thoughts, like the glitter in the jar, are settled and their mind is clear.

MANTRAS FOR QUIET MIND

+ *My mind is quiet, my mind is clear.*

+ *Each breath clears my mind.*

+ *In this moment my mind is still.*

+ *My mind clears like a cloud lifting.*

+ *I have the ability to quiet my mind.*

Empathy

Empathy allows us to be able to imagine what others are going through and what they are feeling. This is the foundation of kindness, compassion, and consideration. Although we are born with the capacity for empathy, it is a learned trait; we need to be shown how to be empathetic.

Although raising an empathic child is something people have always strived to do, I can't think of a time when we have needed empathy and kindness more than right now. There is so much hurt, pain, and struggle in the world and it seems like instead of listening to each other and practicing empathy, we are all just yelling and looking at one another as an enemy.

To share empathy with our children, we need to model it for them, which means that we need to first look for it within ourselves.

Do we take time to be empathetic with our children, our family, and those around us? Since we know that our kids learn this trait from us, it is worth taking some time to reflect on what lessons we are teaching them about empathy.

However, on the flip side, for anyone who is a highly sensitive person or has a highly sensitive child, like I do, you also know that experiencing deep levels of empathy can be a tricky thing to navigate. Some of us are deep feelers, and that is beautiful. I see this in Porkchop, and I can already tell he will have a very high level of empathy, and this may be difficult for him at times. Empathy is about balance, finding it in your heart but not letting it overflow into everything you do.

If you are a deeply empathetic person or you are working with your children to explore empathy, try these meditations. They are three of my favorites for building and maintaining empathy.

Meditation Practices for Empathy

For Adults

Set aside a few minutes to practice this meditation, and come to a comfortable position.

Start to slow your breathing down, following the breath as it dances in and out of your body. Visualize a pink light surrounding your heart, filling you with empathy.

Repeat the following mantras for five minutes or until you feel empathy building in your heart:

- I am a part of the global landscape.
- I welcome empathy into my heart.
- Everyone deserves empathy, including me.
- I see the world from others' perspectives.
- Empathy comes to me easily.

For Kids + Teens

Close your eyes and take a moment to place your hands on your heart to warm up your heart energy.

Visualize loving energy in your heart and see it begin to grow from this place.

Watch the energy grow from your heart, through your body and out into the world, like a web that is moving from your heart center out into the world around you.

See this web stretch out and reach other people, embracing them with your heart's energy and empathy.

Sit and see how you are connected with everyone, and visualize yourself sending your heart's energy to all the people around you.

For Little Ones

For this practice you will need a few slips of paper, something to write with, and a bowl.

Write down a handful of different actions you can do to someone, anything from hitting to playing together to hugging, and place the slips of paper in the bowl.

Have your child take three deep breaths and then take out a piece of paper with an action.

Ask them how this action might make others feel, and how they would feel if someone did this to them.

If they say an action might make someone sad, unhappy, or another negative emotion, ask them what they could do instead to make them feel better. Write that action on the paper and put it back in the bowl.

MANTRAS FOR EMPATHY

+ *I am one with those around me.*

+ *I can see others' perspectives.*

+ *My heart feels for those around me.*

+ *I am an empathetic person.*

+ *Empathy comes to me naturally.*

Comparison

If you've ever found yourself scrolling on social media late at night while you sit on the couch with hair that was last washed a week ago, in a sweatshirt that has either boogers, drool, or spit up on it (you're not sure which), you've probably had a moment where you felt "less." It is easy to feel less when comparing yourself to those perfectly curated online family moments. You know the ones, the snapshots of families with chic coordinating outfits and flawless hair, the effortlessly beautiful family vacations in the Bahamas, the children who look like they never cause a fuss, let alone throw a tantrum.

It's true what they say: Comparison *is* the thief of joy. I never found myself getting sucked into the wheel of comparison harder than my first year of motherhood. I remember looking at other parents both online and in real life and thinking they looked so happy, so put together and so well rested. How did they do it all? And the more that I compared myself to others, the worse I felt about myself.

Remember that the moments you're comparing yourself to tell only part of the story. Social media is designed for sharing a moment, and only a moment. Life is lived in between those moments. Comparison is tricky in part because we are trying to compare a feature film to a highlights reel and in part because we are each telling a different story.

To live in a space of comparison is to always feel better than or less than and to rarely feel content with who we are, what we are doing, and how we are doing it. To release comparison is a radical thing, and it goes against everything that we have been taught. But it is a necessary piece of finding happiness and ease in our lives. Constantly comparing yourself to others is like being a hamster running in a wheel. It just keeps going faster and faster until we can't keep up.

When you're ready to get off the comparison ride—or you want to be ready—try these meditations.

Meditation Practices for Comparison

For Adults

Come to a comfortable position, close your eyes, and take a few deep breaths.

Where are you feeling the sense of comparison in your body? Is it a heaviness in your chest? Is it a clenching in your stomach? Something else?

As you breathe, begin to release the sense of comparison from your body, feel it melt away.

Bring your awareness to your heart center and be flooded with acceptance for who you are and how you show up in life.

Tell yourself three times: *I release my need to compare myself, and I celebrate who I am.*

Visualize yourself being flooded with light, shining, and illuminating who you are, and each unique beautiful part of you.

Sit in this light, allowing yourself to be illuminated for as long as you would like.

For Kids + Teens

Begin by closing your eyes and taking three deep breaths.

Bring your hands to your heart and visualize a pink light of love going into your heart.

Tell yourself three times: *I am one of a kind.*

Let the pink light move through your entire body and into every part of you.

Take three more deep breaths and open your eyes.

Write a list of ways you are unique and what you are good at.

If you like, ask your loved ones to add to the list and hang it somewhere you go often to remind you of how special you are.

For Little Ones

Take your little one outside or to a park where there are plants or flowers growing.

Take time to walk around and look at the flowers and plants, point out their unique beauty, and smell them.

Show your child how each plant and flower is different, and they don't compare themselves to one another or compete, they just grow and let themselves be seen in the light.

Close your eyes, place hands on your hearts, and start sharing the ways in which you and your child are unique and beautiful like the flowers.

MANTRAS FOR COMPARISON

+ *(inhale) Self-acceptance. (exhale) Comparison.*
+ *Every day I walk my own unique path.*
+ *I release my need to compare myself to others.*
+ *I am doing the best I can, and that is plenty.*
+ *My story is worth telling.*

Guilt

Is it just me, or does your capacity to feel guilt only expand with each new member of the family you add? I thought I knew guilt, but then I experienced mom guilt and realized that this was a whole new level.

When I became a mother, I was suddenly flooded with guilty feelings. I felt guilty when my child didn't latch so I had to pump exclusively, then I felt guilty when over a year later I stopped pumping altogether. I felt guilty when I worked, and I felt guilty when my kid ate fries for dinner. I felt guilty when I thought about my life before I had children. I even felt guilty when I accidently washed my family's clothes in lightly scented detergent instead of the normal unscented kind because, what if it made Porkchop's skin itchy? Granted, it never had before, but that didn't stop me from feeling like a bad mom because I was playing fast and loose with *fragranced detergent*.

I was worried about making mistakes that would damage my child, and I found myself constantly looking for ways that I had messed up. I know I'm not the only one who felt this way. I found myself frequently texting my friends about this guilt I was feeling and always got responses like "yeah, me too!" Or "I feel guilty every single day." Or "you're not alone."

These feelings of guilt can feel like the weight of the world bearing down on you, but it's important that you stop, pause, and look at what is happening clearly here. Many things that you may feel guilty for could be out of your control, honest mistakes, or no big deal. Guilt can be an internal compass to let us know when we are stepping off track. But if we internalize it and begin to tell ourselves that we are bad parents or if we start to feel shame for every small little thing, we are stepping onto a slippery slope.

My therapist once stopped me in my tracks when I was talking about feeling guilty for leaving Porkchop when I did my first retreat after maternity leave. I was talking about how bad I felt that I was leaving him, and maybe he wouldn't be connected to me anymore and would forget who I was. And she responded by saying, "Kelly, is what you're saying a thought or a truth? We have many thoughts throughout our day, but not that many truths." Things like "I am a bad mom," or "I am failing my child because I let them eat fries for dinner" are thoughts; they are not truths. The truth is that you are doing the best you can, you are human, and not everything will be perfect—and that does not make you a bad parent.

Defining the difference between truths and thoughts in my own mind has become a powerful tool as I navigate parental guilt. Guilt is often dishonest, and it feeds on our own fears and insecurities, while truths illuminate the situation so you can clearly see what's going on. The next time you or your child experience guilt, stop and ask yourself: *Is this a thought, or is this a truth?* Then use these meditation practice to quell those feelings of guilt.

Meditation Practices for Guilt

For Adults

Begin by taking a few deep breaths and recognizing how you're feeling right in this moment.

Now, name the guilt. Identify what you are feeling guilty for right now, feel it, and breathe.

Visualize your heart opening up. Forgiveness and love are pouring into it, washing away the guilt.

Continue to breathe and allow forgiveness and love to flow through you.

Tell yourself three times: *I forgive myself, I release my guilt, I am a good parent.*

Continue to breathe, allowing love and forgiveness to flow as you repeat this mantra as many times as you need.

For Kids + Teens

Find a quiet place and close your eyes.

Take three deep breaths.

Acknowledge how you're feeling and why you're feeling that way.

Imagine that you have a cup of forgiveness in your hands. It is warm and can taste like anything you like.

As you breathe, imagine yourself drinking your cup of forgiveness. Feel the warmth spread through your body and soothe your guilt.

Continue to breathe and drink your warm cup of forgiveness until you feel better.

For Little Ones

Guilt is likely a new and very uncomfortable emotion for your young ones, so they need a little more guidance to understand what and why they're feeling this way. Use this simple meditation to help talk them through it.

Have them come to a comfortable position, close their eyes, and connect to their hearts.

Ask them to take three deep breaths.

With their eyes closed, ask them the following questions:

- How do you feel?
- Why do you feel this way?
- How can you make it better?

Instruct them to speak to their heart for the answer, and then let them do what their heart is guiding them to do.

MANTRAS FOR GUILT

+ *I release my guilt.*

+ *I am human, I make mistakes, and that is okay.*

+ *I am no longer burdened by my guilt.*

+ *Guilt and shame are released with my breath.*

+ *The weight of guilt is removed from my heart.*

Patience

Waiting for things is hard. It's hard for adults, and it's really hard for children. Patience is a skill that shows up often in my household. I find myself saying "just be patient," frequently, as I attempt to teach Porkchop that you don't need all the things, all the time, right here, immediately. I also find myself having to remember to be patient.

When we are born, the only kind of gratification that you know is instant gratification. You're hungry, you cry, you get your milk. You want a hug, you ask for a hug, you get it. But as we get older, we grow and evolve into a world that doesn't run on instant gratification alone. We must learn patience.

Not only is patience part of life, it can also be a way to show love and empathy for the people we share the world with. When we wait patiently for our children to get their shoes on by themselves—even if it takes longer— we are showing love and giving our kids a chance to grow confidence in their abilities. When we are patient and allow someone who has their hands full to go ahead of us in line, we are sharing love and empathy for other human beings.

In choosing to be patient, we are expressing love on a deeper level and modeling to our children the idea that all will come in good time and that instant isn't always better.

Meditation Practices for Patience

For Adults

Find a comfortable position and, if you'd like, close your eyes.

Bring yourself into this moment by checking in with your senses (what do you see, feel, hear, taste, and smell?).

Allow your awareness to fall on the space just above your lip as you breathe, feeling the cool air move in and the warm air move out.

On the inhale, think *patience*. On the exhale, think *peace*.

Continue to breathe and repeat your mantra as you inhale *patience* and exhale *peace*.

As you do this, welcome patience and peace into your life.

For Kids + Teens

Close your eyes wherever you are and take three deep breaths.

Then, as you breathe normally, tell yourself three times: *I wait patiently.*

Then tell yourself three times, *All will happen when it is supposed to.*

Open your eyes to see if you still feel like you are waiting, and if you are you, repeat this exercise as many times as you need or want.

For Little Ones

Have your child close their eyes and take three deep breaths.

Then have your child think of a time when someone was patient with them and ask them what it felt like. They can describe this feeling or memory out loud to you and talk about what patience feels like.

Now have your child imagine patience like a color, and imagine that color spreading from their heart to people who they want to be patient with.

Any time they need help with patience, have them return to this patience color and focus on it as they breathe.

MANTRAS FOR PATIENCE

+ *(inhale) Patience. (exhale) Frustration.*
+ *In moments of frustration, I embrace patience.*
+ *Breath brings me patience and peace.*
+ *I am able to practice patience in my life.*
+ *Practicing patience comes easy to me.*

Overstimulation

Having spent most of my adulthood as a meditation teacher, I never really suffered from overstimulation. I spent lots of time alone, being quiet, listening to what my body needed, and turning inward and resting my senses.

Then I became a parent.

Let me tell you, I don't think I've had a single moment where I wasn't using at least one of my senses in the last year and half. Since the moment that sweet little Porkchop was pulled from my divine feminine nether regions, I have been constantly surrounded by sounds, my eyes are frequently darting around looking for the next opportunity for my child to injure himself, and I smell things that you don't want me to describe. Perhaps the only sense of mine that isn't being constantly stimulated is my sense of taste, as I inhale my food standing up and don't even remember what I ate.

I frequently found myself feeling "touched out" at night, craving some peace, quiet, and time alone. At first, I thought there was something wrong with me. Why did I just want to be alone at night in my bedroom with dim lights, zoning out until I eventually fell asleep? My senses were on overdrive for almost two years without a break, and it was becoming too much, so my natural inclination was to shut down.

Shortly after what felt like a near nervous breakdown (see the section on "Burnout" for this story, page 105), when I went to my cabin in the woods, I had my first formal experience with forest bathing. This practice involves going out into the forest and just being present and bathing in the energy of the flora and fauna around you.

It was a balm to my overworked senses. I was able to let my eyes just focus on the forest. I breathed the fresh air. I wasn't listening to the sounds of electronic toys, kids screaming, and dogs barking. All I could hear was the breeze through the trees.

Going outside, without any devices, without any kids, without anything but my body and my breath helped me to realize not only how important it was to give my senses a break but just how badly my overstimulation had become. This encouraged me to start taking small overstimulation breaks through meditation, like the practices outlined in this section.

Try these mindfulness practices to soothe your senses when they've been working on overdrive.

Meditation Practices for Overstimulation

For Adults

Go outside, turn off all your devices, and have someone else watch your kids for ten minutes.

Focus on your feet. If possible, stand barefoot on the ground.

Take a few deep breaths and look up. Take in your surroundings.

Allow yourself at least ten minutes to be outside breathing, walking slowly, and giving your mind and senses a break as you just enjoy your surroundings.

For Kids + Teens

Turn off all your devices and go find a quiet and dimly lit space where you can sit, undisturbed, for a few minutes.

Begin to breathe deeply.

Inhale for a count of 4, and exhale for a count of 4.

Repeat this several times.

Close your eyes, if you'd like, and imagine yourself turning inward.

Create a safe space in your mind where you can give your senses a break. Take some time to build this space in your mind: What does it look like? What do you hear? What do you smell? How do you move through the space? This space can be anywhere that you feel safe, and how it looks is completely up to you. Imagine this special place in your mind and stay until you feel ready to return to the here and now.

For Little Ones

Create a sacred space with your child for when they need a break.

Choose a special corner or part of their room and designate it their sacred space.

Decorate it with calm things, dim lights, soothing colors, and comfortable furniture—whatever items or colors make them feel calm—but be careful not to overcrowd or overdecorate. This space should be clean and minimal.

Explain to your child the concept of a sacred space and let them know that any time they need a break they can go to this sacred space to be quiet and alone.

Encourage them to see this space as their peaceful retreat rather than a time out.

MANTRAS FOR OVERSTIMULATION

+ *My body is still, and my mind is quiet.*
+ *I create stillness and peace within.*
+ *I give myself permission to walk away and take breaks.*
+ *One thing at a time.*
+ *Breathe, be, and let go.*

Burnout

We often think of burnout as something that adults experience at work, but the truth is that anyone can experience it in any role. Basically, too much of anything—including parenting—can lead to burnout.

Let's clear something up here: Parental burnout is a real thing, and you are not a bad parent if you experience it.

I'll say it again. Parental burn out is real, and you are not a bad parent if you experience it.

As the primary care provider for Porkchop, I experience parental burnout at times. I'm talking about that chronically tired, worn-down, mind-numbing, soul-sucking kind of overwhelming exhaustion that makes you want to go to bed and wake up a few weeks later after you finally have gotten some time to recharge and be alone.

Just a few weeks ago, I found myself getting to a point where I felt like I was holding on by threads. I was spread way too thin, work was going wild, I was constantly moving from one thing to another, and I had just about had it. Then all it took was one small comment from my husband, and I burst into tears. I began shaking, struggling to speak, and couldn't stop crying. I had finally had it.

It had been so long since I had a break where no one needed me, or was touching me, or expecting anything of me that I finally hit empty. Short of a panic attack, I had never had such an intense and physiological response to anything. I needed a break, and I needed it immediately.

The tough part was that I saw this coming from a mile away. I could feel in my bones that physically, mentally, and emotionally I was barely scraping by, but I didn't take a break sooner because I felt shame for needing one. There is a very powerful narrative in our society that tells us we should always be happy and fulfilled around our family, and that time with our kids should fill our cup. I felt like a failure for not feeling this way, and I was ashamed to admit that I needed a break. So I didn't ask for a break until I was a few steps short of a breakdown.

I did finally ask for my break. Two days later I headed off to a remote cabin on Lake Superior to be quiet, alone, and not in demand for a day and a half. It was exactly what I needed. Finally, some quiet time where I could think! I realized in that moment that I needed to listen to my body and heart when it was saying take a break, step away, and recharge and not to wait until it got this far again.

I spent a lot of time at that cabin thinking and reflecting, and it occurred to me that I had been neglecting my own needs for so long and firing on all cylinders for nearly two years, and enough was enough. I realized that I needed to start taking small moments every day to contribute to my well-being and fill up my cup, and that when Porkchop was older, I would teach him the importance of self-care and daily self-maintenance, too. In other words: The better I take care of myself, the better I can take care of my child.

If you, or one of your children need a break, try these meditation practices to hit the pause button on life.

Meditation Practices for Burnout

For Adults

Give yourself a break from the mental load by going to a quiet place, diming the lights, if possible, and removing all stimuli.

Begin a 4-3-7 breath. Inhale for a count of 4, hold for 3, and exhale for 7.

Do this eight times, then settle into an effortless, natural breath.

Allow yourself five minutes to sit quietly, breathing, and repeat the mantra: *I give myself permission to rest.*

After your five minutes are up, follow this practice with one of your favorite rest practices—whatever that means to you (such as a short walk, a creative pursuit, or time alone with a book), and return to your mantra if you find yourself feeling guilty for taking time to rest.

For Kids + Teens

A mindfulness walk is a great way to reconnect with yourself and fill your cup when you're feeling the crush of burnout. Take your phone in case of emergencies, but try not to check it!

Practice continues on next page

Step outside—barefoot if it is safe to do so. Leave your headphones or earbuds at home, keep your phone in your pocket, and try to limit other distractions.

Take slow steps outside and begin to engage all your senses. Notice what you see, smell, hear, and feel.

Continue to walk, using your senses to notice each moment.

Walk outside until you feel recharged and are ready to return to your daily life.

For Little Ones

This shared breathing exercise is a great way for you and your child to take a break together during a challenging day.

Sit facing your child or lay down beside each other.

Place one hand on your belly and the other on their belly, and have your child do the same to you.

Breathe slowly together, feeling your hands moving up and down, until your breath syncs up.

Breathe together quietly for a minute or two, or as long as you need before returning to your day.

MANTRAS FOR BURNOUT

+ *I give myself permission to take breaks and walk away.*

+ *More is not better.*

+ *My worth is not defined by my productivity.*

+ *Today is today, and tomorrow is tomorrow.*

+ *I ask for help when I need it and take time to rest.*

Intuition

One of the greatest tools I have in my parent toolbox is my intuition. Many times in my life, both before and after having children, I've felt these little nudges, or heard these whispers, or had an unexplained feeling show up and push me in a direction that felt important if not logical. I didn't always realize it in the moment, but that was my intuition guiding me.

We often hear about "mother's intuition," but what about our *human* intuition? I firmly believe that we are all born with the ability to see the unseen or to be able to tap into our intuitive space for guidance and knowledge. Over time, we can become disconnected from our intuition for many different reasons, but we can always reconnect with this sense and rebuild our intuition just like we would reconnect with and rebuild a muscle.

Our intuition is how our highest selves communicate with us and keep us on the right path. It is a protection mechanism, a communication guide, and a direct line to our purest selves.

When we are connected to our intuition, life becomes much easier, as we have the clarity to know when something feels right and when it doesn't. For example, making decisions for your children becomes easier because you can always count on your intuition to lead you. When our children get older and begin to connect with their intuition, they will be able to tap into their guidance as well.

Connecting with your intuition is like developing a friendship. You start by getting to know one another, and then it grows into a deeper trust and bond. Before you know it, the two of you will be good friends, in clear communication all the time, walking through life in lockstep. The following meditations are ways that you can connect with your intuition and open the line of communication.

Meditation Practices for Intuition

For Adults

Give yourself permission to take a few minutes of quiet for yourself.

Slow down your breath and open a connection with your intuition.

Tell yourself three times, *I am connected to my intuition. I know what is best for me and my family.*

In your mind's eye, imagine a silver drop of light illuminating the space between your eyebrows.

Visualize this silver light illuminating and awakening your intuition. With each passing moment, the light grows stronger, and your intuition grows stronger too.

Tell yourself 3 more times: *I am connected with my intuition, I know what is best for me and my family.*

Stay with this silver light at your brow for as long as you would like.

Repeat this often to keep your intuition strong.

For Kids + Teens

Come to a comfortable position and close your eyes.

Focus on the space between your eyebrows and begin to practice alternate nostril breathing.

Do five rounds of Alternate Nostril Breathing (page 31), focusing on the space between your eyebrows.

After the fifth round, release your hands to your lap and breathe normally.

Tell yourself three times: *I trust my intuition.*

As you breathe, imagine the breath is going up across your eyebrows awakening your intuition and allowing you to clearly understand what it says.

Breathe across your third eye for three to five minutes.

Close your meditation by repeating three times: *I trust my intuition.*

For Little Ones

Have your child sit quietly and breathe in for 4 and out for 4. Repeat this 4 times.

Ask your child to "talk to their gut" by ask them a question like, "What does your gut want to do today?"

Then while they are quiet and connected have them tell you "what their gut says."

Have them practice their intuition throughout the day by asking a question and saying, "What does your gut say?" and have them reflect on what their intuition's answer is.

MANTRAS FOR INTUITION

+ *I am connected to my intuition.*

+ *I follow my intuition.*

+ *My intuition guides me in the right direction.*

+ *I trust my gut.*

+ *Intuitive guidance surrounds me.*

Resilience

Life is full of ups and downs. Sometimes we get knocked down, struggle, or fail. Resilience isn't about finding a way to avoid failure or about being tough as nails and devoid of feelings. It's the practice of being able to pick ourselves back up after we've been knocked down or after we've gone through a period of struggle, all while keeping a certain softness of heart.

Your resilience is like a rubber band. When you get stretched, you snap back, even if that snap back can be a bit intense at times. If you ask the rubber band to stretch again and again and again, it will eventually start to grow in size, and the snap back won't be as intense or painful. When we, or our children experience a setback or struggle, we are being stretched and snapped, and with each stretching and snapping we become softer, more fluid. We start to grow.

For me, the struggle with trying to raise a resilient child is the realization that I will have to watch him struggle, be challenged, and most likely experience pain of some sort. I will have to let go of his tiny little hand and allow him to make mistakes and fail. Although I can act as a safety net for him if he falls, I can't hover over him for all of his life removing every challenge or obstacle that comes in his way.

To love someone sometimes means you have to let them struggle, walk their own path, and fail. You can be there to help put the pieces back together or cheer them on along the way, but sometimes love means removing the training wheels and letting go of the bike so our loved ones find their balance on their own.

Although our initial response to a setbacks or disappointments may be negative, mindfulness asks us to look at our situation without judgment, to search for the lesson and the blessing in every moment, even the ones that are hard. If we look at each challenge as moment to stretch and grow, we will begin to build up our ability to bounce back from failures big and small. Eventually, we will find resilience within ourselves.

Try these meditation practices to connect to or grow your resilience the next time you are going through a period of struggle.

Meditation Practices for Resilience

For Adults

Come to a quiet place and make sure all distractions are turned off.

Take a quick scan of the body to check in on how you're feeling.

Begin to breathe deeply, sending breath to all your cells.

As you breathe, sit with your feelings. How are you feeling right now during this time of struggle and challenge?

Continue to breathe deeply, and see yourself growing, expanding, and evolving from this change.

Ask yourself, what is this moment teaching me? Where is the blessing?

Reflect on what you are learning from this struggle as you continue to breathe and send love to yourself for several minutes.

Seal your meditation by visualizing yourself bouncing back from this time of struggle stronger, more resilient, and ready for the next challenge.

For Kids + Teens

Find a quiet place where you can meditate for a few minutes.

Begin by imagining that you are a tree in the ground.

See your roots growing down into the soil.

See your branches, trunk, and leaves.

Watch as a storm passes through, knocking off branches and leaves and making your trunk sway.

Once the storm has passed, visualize yourself recovering from the storm with the trunk getting thicker, the roots going deeper, and the leaves coming back larger and stronger.

Stay with the meditation for several minutes, or until you feel you have tapped into your inner strength and resilience.

For Little Ones

If your child is feeling let down after a setback, or is experiencing a challenge, teach them how to breathe deeply and repeat these phrases as many times as they need:

I am strong.
I can do hard things.
I am learning something new.
Failure is a chance to learn.

MANTRAS FOR RESILIENCE

+ *I can do hard things.*

+ *Resilience is abundant within me.*

+ *Challenges are an opportunity to learn and grow.*

+ *I build resilience each day.*

+ *I do not give up; instead, I learn and grow.*

Connecting with the True Self

If there was one section in this book that I could pull out and spend hours talking about, it would be this one. When people ask me what I do, I often tell them that I help people connect with their true selves through yoga, meditation, and introspection.

The reason that I feel so strongly about this topic is because I believe the secret to living a truly joyful and fulfilling life is living from the true self space. The true self, depending on what you believe, can take many forms. It can be the soul, your essence, the divine within, atman, you name it. What all these terms are trying to describe is that part of you that you are born with—the part of you that just is. It may be easier to see this in your children than yourself at first. Think about those funny little quirks, personality traits, preferences that your children has almost from the moment they are born. This is their true self.

As we continue through life, we sometimes become disconnected from who we really are. We may eventually find ourselves losing this part of us that feels like our "true self," making us feel lost in our own skin. Society starts to tell us how to be, what is good, what is bad, and what happiness should be. But no matter how disconnected from the true self you feel now, don't worry, because you can always find your way back.

Our true selves are like due north on a compass. They help us to stay on track and go in the right direction when we walk our journey of life. The true self is pure, authentic, and good. When you begin to connect to your true self, a few things will happen. You will get to know yourself on a deeper level than ever before, you will be able to reach out to this space for guidance, and you will begin to access a space of happiness.

When you live from your true self, things just feel right, and you know deep down that you are doing what is right for you. Your children are probably still connected to this space if they are young. That's beautiful; honor it, nurture it, and let them light to way for you on how to live authentically and from this space. Connect with this space on a personal level when you are trying to make a hard decision on behalf of yourself or your young children. I found my true self to be particularly helpful when I was making decisions like, *Am I done breastfeeding?* Or, *What do I really value as a parent?* It helped me drown out a lot of the noise that surrounded me during those first few years of parenting.

Try these meditation practices if you want to connect with your true self and see what it may have to say.

Meditation Practices for Connecting with the True Self

For Adults

Find a quiet place to meditate.

Begin belly breathing.

Now see yourself traveling inward, away from the external world and into a safe space within.

In this safe space you meet your true self. Visualize what they look like. Is your true self a person? Or a ball of light? Or something else? There is no wrong answer; just trust your gut and visualize what your true self looks like.

Sit with your true self, talk to them, get to know them, embrace them.

When you feel connected to this space, you can ask questions, if you'd like, and perhaps receive guidance.

End your meditation by sending love to your true self.

For Kids + Teens

Come to a comfortable position and, if you'd like, close your eyes.

Take a few deep breaths, and then settle into an effortless rhythm of breath.

Visualize yourself sitting on a beach at sunrise.

Slowly watch the sunrise, and let it move over your entire body.

See the sunshine on your body and feel it illuminate your soul, your true self.

Look clearly at your true self and send it love.

Spend time sitting on this beach, sparkling in sunlight and getting to know your soul until you feel you have connected with this space.

For Little Ones

Have fun and let your kids show you who their true selves are with some mindful art. You will probably end up with a masterpiece on your hands and learn some new things about your kids, too. You'll need some art supplies, such as paper and crayons or watercolors.

Ask your kids about their true selves/soul (or any other name you have for it). Talk to them about the idea of their true self, and the part of them that it beautiful and unique. You can use any word for this that you like— maybe "soul" or "your one-of-a-kind self."

Then ask them to create a picture of their true selves and to name all the things that this true self likes.

MANTRAS FOR TRUE SELF

+ *I am connected to my true self.*

+ *I live from my soul space.*

+ *My true self is beautiful.*

+ *My true self illuminates my path.*

+ *I allow my soul to be seen, and I live from this space.*

Self-Love

Plato once said, "Be kind, for everyone you meet is fighting a hard battle."

I, like many women, have struggled with self-love throughout my life. I struggled to feel like I was smart enough, thin enough, or beautiful enough. If I'm being completely honest, I still struggle with loving myself sometimes. And after I became a mother, it became even more difficult.

A few weeks after giving birth, I looked at my body and didn't recognize the person I was looking at. My eyes were heavy from sleepless nights, my hair was beginning to turn gray and fall out, and creases were starting to form in my forehead. I was struggling every day to feel like a good enough mom to Porkchop, and I found myself wondering who I even was anymore. Without my career, the international travel, working seventy- to eighty-hour weeks building my business and growing my podcast, I felt like I didn't have an identity. I felt empty and sad.

But that all changed one day when I was rocking Porkchop to sleep. He was refusing to sleep anywhere but in my arms, rocking. So instead of doing all the countless things I felt like I needed to do that day, I was sitting in a chair, holding him, and rocking him while he slept. And while I sat there, rocking him for hours, I cried. I cried because I felt like a failure who didn't even brush her teeth until noon. I responded to emails and texts days or weeks later. I couldn't even get my baby to sleep in a crib. I sat there, rocking my baby, crying, thinking about everything that I did wrong, all that was bad about me, and what a big fat failure I was.

But then I looked down at my sweet, precious sleeping baby. I looked at his sleeping face, and so much love poured out of me for him.

And then it hit me.

He was made from me. How could I love him unconditionally, and so fiercely, but be so cruel and unkind to myself? It's not like I was looking down at him and thinking I love all the parts of you that came from your dad and I hate everything that you got from me. No, I *loved* him. Without question, without thought, and without conditions.

To love my child was to love myself. That moment right there changed the way that I looked at self-love. Porkchop loved me without question, and I loved him without question. We came from the same body, and if I was going to teach him how to practice self-love, I would have to learn it for myself first.

I still have moments when I cry, feel like a failure, and wonder who I am now that I am a mother. But through it all, I send myself love—just like I would send my son when he has moments of doubt or struggle. If you or one of your family members are experiencing one of these moments, try these meditations.

Meditation Practices for Self-Love

For Adults

Come to a comfortable position, turn off distractions, and close your eyes.

Begin belly breathing.

On the inhale think "I love myself" and on the exhale think" I love my family."

As you do this, visualize a pink light of self-love washing over you, pouring into every cell, every inch of your being.

As you see this pink light pouring through you, feel yourself filling up with that same unconditional love you give others, but send it to yourself.

Do this for several minutes. When you're ready, close your meditation by saying *I am worthy, I am enough, I love myself.*

For Kids + Teens

Come to a comfortable position.

Take three deep breaths, breathing in through your nose and out through your mouth.

Now tell yourself three times: *I love and accept myself.*

Visualize your body and name three things that you love about your body. I know this might be hard, but you can do it!

Visualize your mind and name three great ideas you have.

Visualize your heart and name three things you love about who you are.

End your meditation by telling yourself three times *I love and accept myself.*

For Little Ones

Have your child sit with you and take three deep breaths.

Now have them place their hands on their heart to warm up their feelings of love in their heart.

Explain to your child that you are going to fill up a love tank. Just like when you go to the gas station to fill up your car, you can fill up your heart with love.

Give an example of filling up your love tank by saying something that you love about yourself, and then say something that you love about them.

Tell your child to fill up their "love tank" and, as they breathe, say things that they love about themselves.

Take turns breathing and saying what you love about yourselves until you have each said ten things and your tanks are full.

MANTRAS FOR SELF-LOVE

+ *Self-love comes to me easily.*

+ *I love who I am unconditionally.*

+ *I give myself permission to love who I am and honor my needs.*

+ *I start my day with practices of self-love.*

+ *My body deserves love and respect.*

Energy

We're all tired sometimes. Maybe you were up late with the baby, or you had a big deadline at work, or perhaps you're just juggling all the things all of the time.

Although we normally think about meditation as a calming, introverting practice, you can also use meditation and breath to give yourself a little boost. Like a mindful shot of espresso to your body and mind. Although meditation on its own can help to mentally stimulate you and wake up your brain, combining breath with a little gentle movement is one of the best ways to get an energy boost when you need it.

Pranayama, which is the Sanskrit term for breathwork is made up of the two words *prana* and *yama*. Prana means vitality or life force, and yama means control, which translates "pranayama" into "the control of life force or energy." In other words, by using our breath we can manipulate our energy in meaningful ways. We also know that taking small movement breaks throughout the day can help boost both our energy and mood.

When you or your little ones need an energy boost, try these three breath-work and mindful movement practices.

Meditation Practices for Energy

For Adults

Find a clear space where you can sit or stand without bumping into anything.

Whether you are sitting or standing, create a long spine, shoulders softened and melting down your back, and spine long so you can breathe with ease.

Begin to tune in to your breath, letting it become slow and deep.

On an inhale, sweep your hands out, up and over your head until they touch.

On the exhale, bend your elbows and create goalpost arms with a small backbend.

On the next inhale, reach back up.

On the next exhale, take your hands to heart center.

Repeat this ten times or until you feel a shift in your energy that tells you that you're ready to go.

For Kids + Teens

Begin this practice by taking a few deep breaths, connecting with your inhale and exhale.

Begin the three-part breath technique and repeat it ten times.

If you would like to add movement, first make sure you have enough space to fully extend your arms out to the side. As you inhale, raise your hands out to your sides. On each of your three inhales, raise your hands higher until they meet over your head. On the exhale, move them down through heart center. Repeat.

After your ten repetitions, close your eyes and find stillness and notice if you are feeling more awake after this meditation.

For Little Ones

Have your child begin by checking in with their bodies. Ask them which parts feel sleepy.

Have your child start to connect with their breath.

On the inhale, instruct your child to send energy to the sleepy parts of their body.

On the exhale, tell them to move the sleepy part of the body any way they like, such as shake it, wave it, sway, or make circles.

Repeat this until all the sleepy parts have "woken up."

MANTRAS FOR ENERGY

+ *I am filled with an abundance of energy.*
+ *Energy flows through me with ease.*
+ *My body is energized and strong.*
+ *My mind is awake and clear.*
+ *I welcome energy to flow within me.*

Courage

Let's start by clearing up another common misconception: Having courage doesn't mean that you aren't afraid. It means continuing forward even though you *are* afraid. Many aspects of life will ask us to call upon our courage. When we become parents, we need courage. When we stand up for something we believe in or speak our truth, we need courage. When we choose to love ourselves, we need courage.

To live an authentic and fulfilling life, we must hold fear with one hand and courage with the other. Life is scary. Change is scary. Being a parent is scary. There are a lot of scary things out there, and it would be easy to lock ourselves away, never interact with other people, or to hold our children tight and never let them venture out into the big, scary world around us. To live, we need to have courage.

For me, courage, trust, and fear live together in a constant ebb and flow state. We experience fear, we call forward our courage, and then we trust that our courage will be enough to get us through. Courage isn't enacted by force or aggression or in loud over-the-top ways—those often are expressions of fear—but instead asks us to open our hearts, speak our truth, and allow ourselves to be seen in the daylight, even when that feels scary.

My son is a deep feeler. Although this is something that is beautiful and unique to his spirit, I know that one day navigating life as someone who feels things so deeply might be scary. It will require that he have an honest and courageous heart as he navigates the ups and downs of life. I hope that as he grows he learns that courage can take many forms—sometimes soft, sometimes kind, sometimes bold. No matter what form courage takes, it is the vessel that will help him stay afloat in the tumultuous waters of fear, and trust is the wind that will bolster his sails.

Courage comes from within. When you need to tap into this space, try these meditations to ignite your spark of courage.

Meditation Practices for Courage

For Adults

Find a comfortable position and a quiet place to reflect on what you need courage for right now.

Allow the external world to fall away as you turn inward.

Connect with your courage, whatever that feels like for you. Begin to feel into this space inside you and visualize what it looks like.

Now call your courage forward and ask it to be present in your life.

As you call your courage forward, feel the sensation of courage begin to move and hum throughout your body.

Sit with the quiet, steady strength of your courage.

Seal your meditation by taking three deep breaths and then thank your courage for coming forward.

For Kids + Teens

Take a few deep breaths.

Slow down your breath, place your hands on your chest, and feel the beat of your heart begin to slow down and become steady.

Visualize a spark of courage in your heart, like a birthday candle or a sparkler.

Continue to breathe deeply and watch as this flicker of light becomes larger and brighter.

As the light grows, your courage grows too.

Take ten breaths here with this light, and let it become strong.

Tell yourself three times: *I am brave, I am courageous, I am strong.*

For Little Ones

Have your child get two stuffed animals, dolls, or any other "friends" they may have.

One stuffed animal will be a worry doll, and the other will be the courage doll.

Have your child begin by holding the worry doll. Encourage them to share all their worries and fears with this doll. The doll will hold on to their worries, so they no longer have to experience that fear.

Next, have your child hold the courage doll. Have the child take three deep breaths and instruct them "fill" up this doll with courage with each breath.

Tell your child that anytime they need a courage boost, they can hug this doll and they will activate their courage. And remind them that they can also always go to an adult they trust.

MANTRAS FOR COURAGE

+ *I have an abundance of strength within me.*

+ *I can access my courage anytime I need it.*

+ *In moments of fear, I am filled with strength.*

+ *Courage flows through me with ease.*

+ *I am courage, I am strong, I am powerful.*

Anger

I know this might be somewhat controversial, but I don't think anger is always a bad thing.

Yes, anger can lead to horrible things. It can cause outbursts, frustration, and actions that we may regret later if we let our anger boil over and take control of us. But on the flip side, anger can tell us when we have been violated or wronged. It can tell us that someone has crossed a boundary. It can come from a space of deep passion or even justice. Life is not always sunshine, love, and unicorns. Sometimes people make us angry. Sometimes we are treated badly. And sometimes we are just mad.

I remember I had a lot of anger in my first year of motherhood. I couldn't even really tell you what I was angry about, but boy, was I angry. I had a short fuse; small things could set me off and at the drop of a hat, I could boil over. At first, I wanted to push this anger down. I wanted to hide it deep down within me where no one could see it. I could put a smile on my face, pretend like it was all okay, and keep my cool even when I was filled with rage, but that only worked for so long.

One night after boiling over and snapping at my entire family, I tried sitting with this feeling. I tried my best not to judge how I was feeling or label if it was good or bad; I just sat in meditation and asked questions about my anger. Why was I angry? Why did I want to hide it? Did I feel someone had wronged me? What triggered my anger? As I sat with this feeling of anger, I became comfortable with it, looked it right in the eye, and got clear on where my anger was coming from and why. Once I was clear, I could start working on it.

Being inquisitive and curious about the anger that you're experiencing can help you identify what is causing it, and what you need to do to move past it if you choose.

The problem with anger isn't that we feel it but that we are in a constant push and pull with it, wanting to hide it, wash it away, and pretend it never existed. Instead, we should sit and get comfortable with this uncomfortable feeling and let it reveal a deeper part of ourselves. It may deepen our capacity to feel, understand, and ultimately act with compassion and love.

The following meditations are my favorites if you want to sit with your anger and peel back the layers of this complex emotion.

Meditation Practices for Anger

For Adults

Find a comfortable position and do six rounds of Box Breath (page 32).

Focus on being with your feelings.

Sit with your anger and let it be present in you and pour through you.

Ask yourself, *Why am I feeling anger?*

Then ask yourself, *What is my anger telling me about myself?*

Reflect on these questions as you breathe. Try not to judge how you are feeling.

If you would like to remove your anger, imagine that with every exhale, puffs of smoke like a dragon leave your body, releasing your red-hot feelings of anger with it.

Continue to visualize the smoke leaving your body until all your anger has been released.

For Kids + Teens

Take a moment to check in with where you're feeling the anger.

Take a few deep breaths, and as you exhale allow the angry parts of your body to soften.

Now visualize a glass sphere in your hands.

As you breathe, imagine that the glass is pulling your anger out through your hands, and it is being trapped inside the sphere.

Give your anger a color and watch the sphere turn that color as you continue to breathe and allow the anger to be pulled and removed from your body.

End your meditation by visualizing this sphere being buried in the ground where it will be recycled by the earth and turned into love.

For Little Ones

When your child is angry, have them stop and inhale counting from 1 to 3 and exhale counting down from 3 to 1.

Then have them say why they are angry and where they feel the anger in their body.

Then ask your child how they want to remove that anger from that place. Give them some examples: a light melts it, someone takes it away in a box, or a hug removes it.

Have them visualize that their anger is being removed from their body however it feels best to them, as they breath in for 3 and out for 3.

MANTRAS FOR ANGER

+ *(inhale) Acceptance. (exhale) Anger.*
+ *I release my anger.*
+ *I accept how I feel and honor my story.*
+ *This moment is temporary; I breathe and it will pass.*
+ *Anger does not define me.*

Nightmares

It isn't fully known what causes nightmares in children, but when your child has a nightmare it can be a scary experience for everyone. It is believed that many nightmares are due to stress or being overtired. Although we may not be able to cure them, we can use practices like deep breathing, progressive muscle relaxation, and visualization to help soothe our children—and us—when they happen.

Using traditional techniques for relaxation can help you fall back asleep after a nightmare by soothing the sympathetic nervous system. After a nightmare, you may experience a rapid heartbeat. You may be sweating and finding it hard to calm down. This is your sympathetic nervous system reacting to the experience you just had and, before you can fall back asleep, you need to try to reverse it.

You can teach your children relaxation techniques, or you can talk to them about their nightmares, and develop some visualizations to help them. For example, they might want to imagine a protective bubble around them so the scary things in their nightmares can't get them. Maybe you place a crystal or other object on their nightstand to "absorb" the nightmares. Ask your kids to trust their gut on what they need, and honor that. Whatever you can think of to help soothe them, give it a try.

All three of the following meditation and visualization practices can easily be modified and used for any age group, based on what they need help with at night.

Meditation Practices for Nightmares

Adults

Take a moment to resettle into bed, and give yourself permission to feel any feelings of fear, panic, or discomfort you may be experiencing.

Begin the Relaxation Breath.

On each exhale, visualize yourself walking down a staircase, becoming more relaxed and tired with each step down.

Exhale again, stepping down another step and getting closer to sleep.

Keep breathing and imagine that you're walking down a staircase every time you exhale, moving closer and closer toward relaxation and sleep until you eventually drift off.

For Kids + Teens

Flip your pillow over and make any other changes you need to feel comforted and secure (maybe pull your blanket over your head or hug a pillow or stuffed animal).

Begin to slow down your breath.

Focus on the nostrils as the air moves in and out through the nose.

Imagine that you are lying in bed with a beautiful full moon above you.

The moonlight starts shining on your feet, warming and relaxing them.

Then it moves to your shins, and slowly moves over your entire body relaxing it, warming it, and soothing it.

Once the moon has softened your entire body, continue to breathe and repeat to yourself until your body and mind drift back to sleep: *I am safe, I am calm, now is the time for sleep.*

Little Ones

When your child comes to you with a nightmare, first ask them what scared them about their nightmare and reaffirm to them that they are safe.

When they are ready to get back to bed, have them visualize a bubble of light surrounding them (any color that feels right works). Nothing scary or bad can come in through this bubble. Inside it, they are safe.

Have them take ten deep breaths. With every exhale, this bubble grows bigger. They can expand the bubble all the way to the corners of their room if they choose.

Have them visualize this bubble around them, protecting them and keeping them safe for as long as they want, until they're ready to go back to sleep.

If they would like, have them continue to expand the bubble beyond them and all the way around the house, keeping everyone and everything within it safe and sound.

MANTRAS FOR NIGHTMARES

+*I sleep peacefully at night.*

+*My body is relaxed, and I fall asleep with ease.*

+*I am not afraid of my dreams.*

+*Nightmares do not impact my sleep.*

+*I accept that my nightmares are not real, and I sleep soundly.*

Compassion

One of my favorite quotes from the Dalai Lama is: "if you want others to be happy, practice compassion. If you want to be happy, practice compassion."

Is there truly anything in this world that feels more loving and warm than compassion?

I've found myself thinking about compassion a lot. Not just because I want to raise a consciously compassionate child, but because I sometimes wonder if we as humans are losing our ability to have compassion altogether.

Sometimes I struggle not to think about all the sadness, anger, and hate that seems to fill our world. When I really stop to think about the world I'm living in—one with school shootings, hateful conflicts, war, poverty, and rights being stripped away from some and withheld from others—it makes me question if true compassion really exists. Then I wonder how I could possibly make a difference when all the problems seem so big.

The problems are big. They're huge, actually. And it seems that no one really has the answers. So sometimes when I hold Porkchop and rock him to sleep at night, I kiss his little head and send a prayer to anyone who will answer to keep him safe and to open all of our hearts so we can start showing compassion to one another again, instead of being stuck in an endless cycle of hate, rage, and pain.

When I think about everything that is happening in the world, it seems overwhelming and like I can't do anything to change it. But that isn't true. Although I can't fully heal and repair the damage of the world, I can share compassion with people I come into contact with each day and also teach my child how to be compassionate.

By opening my heart and sharing compassion with those around me and with myself, I give encourage those around me to do the same. It is my hope that the compassion that sparks from my heart will spread like a web throughout my community and ultimately to the greater world. This may seem like great expectations for small acts, but even the greatest fires begin from a single spark. You never know. Taking a moment to show compassion to those around you may be the spark that sets the world ablaze.

When you want to boost your compassion or teach your children how to show compassion, try these three meditations.

Meditation Practices for Compassion

For Adults

Find a comfortable position. Sit tall, creating a long spine, and place your hands over your heart to connect with your compassion.

Soften your shoulders and let go of any areas where you feel squeezing or clenching in your body.

Take a few moments to follow your breath as you turn inward.

Bring your awareness to your heart center. See a green light surrounding it.

Continue to breathe and allow this green light to spread from your heart throughout your entire body.

As you visualize this green light of compassion spreading through you, repeat the following mantras to yourself.

- May I be happy.
- May I be healthy.
- May I love unconditionally.
- May I be filled with joy and peace.
- May I be filled with compassion.

Seal your meditation by radiating compassion to yourself and all of those in your life.

Kids + Teen

Begin your practice by taking a few deep breaths.

Place your hands on your heart, and tune in to the feeling of compassion. Explore the feeling of compassion by thinking of someone or something that you love and share kindness with—perhaps a friend, family member, or pet.

Focus on the feelings of compassion that you feel for this person, pet or thing and let that feeling move through you.

Visualize your compassion and kindness as a bubble of your favorite color growing from your heart and surround you.

Imagine this bubble growing and expanding until it is so big that it extends a few feet in front of you, so anyone who encounters you today will feel this compassion and kindness.

Continue to visualize this bubble growing bigger and bigger until it surrounds the entire world, filling it with your kindness and compassion.

End your meditation by saying three times: *All people deserve compassion.*

Little Ones

Grab some blocks or other objects your child can stack.

Tell them that each block represents a way to be nice and compassionate to someone (including themselves!).

Get the activity started by giving them an example of a way to show compassion and put down the first block.

Now it's your child's turn. Ask them about some ways they can be kind and compassionate to others (e.g., sharing toys, asking what they like, holding hands, petting the dog gently). For every new idea, stack another block on the tower.

When they have said as many things as they can think, point out how large their stack has become and praise them for having so many good ideas.

Have them work on "building their tower" mentally each day through their actions.

Remember to praise them when you notice them demonstrating compassion.

MANTRAS FOR COMPASSION

+ *My heart recognizes the heart in all beings.*

+ *I am filled with compassion.*

+ *I give myself compassion each day.*

+ *Compassion comes to me easily.*

+ *I lovingly hold space for myself and others.*

CH 4

Meditations for a
Growing Family

As you raise your family, there may be times when you are not only parenting your current child but expecting another. When I was pregnant with Porkchop, I found meditation to be one of the best tools I had for navigating the experience. In fact, I found it so helpful that I started a second podcast called *Meditation Mama*, where I share my prenatal meditations with other women who were expecting.

I found out I was pregnant in March 2020 and not even a week later stay-at-home orders went into place. Suddenly I was sicker than I had ever been in my life, my business on hold for the foreseeable future, and I was stuck inside an 800-square-foot apartment with my partner. This wasn't exactly what I had expected with my pregnancy. Where was the glow everyone talked about? Where were the lovely walks outside showing off my bump, or seeing the look on everyone's face when I told them I was pregnant? At the beginning of my pregnancy, I was a bit of a mess and everything felt like it had been turned upside down.

So when everything felt lost and I wasn't sure what to do, I did what I always do during times of uncertainty. I returned to my center, and I relied on meditation. I used a daily meditation practice to quiet my mind, quell my anxiety, and send love to the little being inside of me day after day. In fact, meditation was part of my pregnancy journey even before I conceived Porkchop, when I started doing soul baby meditations and mentally preparing myself to become a parent.

Although every pregnancy is unique, and each woman will experience this time in her life differently, I found meditation to be a useful tool from the moment I decided I was ready to be a mom to the day that I delivered Porkchop. In this chapter, I will share the benefits of meditating during pregnancy, the best positions for meditating while pregnant, and seven of my personal favorite prenatal meditations that I used while growing my family.

I hope that while you use these meditations you remember to be gentle with yourself, be kind, and use these few minutes a day to honor your body and nourish that growing little being within. Give yourself permission to feel however you want to feel, to experience whatever you experience, to give yourself grace as you give life, and to walk this path together with your baby.

Why Prenatal Meditation?

Not only is meditation a wonderful tool to use to connect with your baby, quiet your body and mind, and reduce stress during your pregnancy, studies have also show that meditating while pregnant benefits women in the following ways (Dhillon, 2017).

- Reduces the mother's stress, anxiety, and depression.
- Lowers heart rate and blood pressure.
- Improves sleep quality and duration.
- Increases feelings of connection to baby.
- Reduces labor fears and anxiety.
- May decrease premature birth.
- May help decrease pain during labor.

Personally, I found meditation to be a great time for me to check in each day with myself and my baby and to find small moments of quiet and peace to be alone with my little one. No matter what your goal is with meditation, keeping your practice (or starting one) during pregnancy can be a great way to support yourself during this time.

Meditation Positions for Pregnancy

If this isn't your first child, then you probably know that one of the most annoying things about being pregnant is that you can't get comfortable. Your back might hurt, it might be hard to get down on the floor, you may not be able to lay on your stomach or back anymore, or you may find yourself constantly breathless, as if you just ran around the block when all you did was try to put your pants on.

For some, traditional meditation positions may work throughout their entire pregnancy. If this is not you (it wasn't me), here are some prenatal meditation positions you may find helpful as your body changes and your baby grows.

Side Lying Position

- Lay on your side on a couch or in your bed.
- Place a pillow under your head and between your knees, or use a pregnancy pillow if you have one.
- Optional, add a pillow under your belly to help support the baby.
- Cover yourself with a blanket if you get cold.

Seated Position with Elevated Hips

Sitting on the floor may not be ideal after a certain point in your pregnancy. Try adding a pillow or a meditation cushion to elevate the hips or sitting in a chair.

Reclined "Queen's Throne" Position

- Take a few pillows from your bed and place them under your back to prop up your torso so it is elevated.
- Lay yourself back on the pillows, and stretch your legs out long, or for low back support bend the knees and place your feet on the ground.
- Let your hands rest on baby or fall out to the side.
- An optional variation of this is to sit in a recliner and lean back to meditate.

Guided Meditations for Pregnancy

Soul Baby

A warning here, where I am about to go might seem a bit "out there," but hear me out. This guided practice helps you welcome the soul of your baby into your body through guided visualization. I did this practice when I was ready to become a mother and have since led hundreds of women through it when they were trying to conceive. I believe it works.

Think of this meditation as mentally preparing your body and mind for the little one you are welcoming in, as if you were preparing your womb for a long-term house guest, and then opening your heart and telling that baby you are ready for them. If you were going to have a visitor over at your house you would probably pick up a little bit, prepare the space, make sure everything was good to go, and then open the front door and tell them to come in, right?

You can use this practice when you are ready to welcome a new baby into your life or when you are trying to get pregnant. Repeat this practice as many times as you would like; keep an open mind, and approach it from a space of love for your body and your future child.

Guided Practice

- Give yourself permission to release expectations, open your heart, and allow yourself to feel whatever comes up for you during this practice.

- Close your eyes, if you'd like, and focus on your breath.

- Begin belly breathing.

- Let your awareness fall on your womb and focus your attention there.

- Visualize your womb becoming repaired, rejuvenated, healthy, and ready to hold and grow new life.

- Continue to visualize this healing for as long as you would like, until it feels like it is complete.

- Then in the center of your womb, visualize an opalescent light, like sparkling moonstone shining in all directions, bringing life, vitality, energy, and love to your womb space, continuing to prepare it for new life, and a new pregnancy.

- Open your heart and fill it with the love you have for your children, both present and those you are welcoming in. Let your heart overflow with love, and send that love down to your womb space.

- Welcome in the soul of your next baby. State in your mind or out loud, "I am ready for you, baby, you can come whenever you are ready."

- With your heart, visualize the soul and life of your next baby coming into your world, into your heart, and into your womb space, filling it with unconditional love.

- Stay here, loving and welcoming this future baby for as long as you would like.

Prenatal Body Love

The body changes a lot during pregnancy. There are obvious changes, like your belly getting bigger, your ankles getting puffy and swollen, or your boobs starting to feel like cement-filled cantaloupes. And then there are the less obvious changes, like your saliva getting thicker, your body growing an entirely new organ, and your hair ceasing to shed. Although these changes are completely natural, that doesn't mean that they are always easy.

One of my biggest struggles during pregnancy was with the changes in my body. I found myself in this constant push and pull between the changes in my body and learning how to accept those changes.

For me, one of the greatest tools that meditation gives us is the ability to objectively look at what is happening around us and within is. Through meditation, I was able to take inventory of how I was feeling each day physically, mentally, and emotionally, without judgment. I was able to tune in to what my body, my mind, and my heart were saying about the changes, and then practice a meditation based on the feedback I was getting. Time and time again, I found myself wanting to send love to my new body and honor the process it was going through.

The following guided meditation is the one I used when I needed to send a little TLC to my physical self. I hope it helps you as well.

Guided Practice

- Take a few moments to get comfortable and quiet your mind.
- Feel your body, check in with how it is doing, and send breath to all your cells.
- Check in with each part of your body one at a time, think about what it does for you each day, and send love and gratitude to each part.
- Feel the beat of your heart, and experience gratitude for every single beat that is sustaining you and your baby together.
- Feel your feet and legs, and thank them for holding you up every day.
- Move up to your hips, pelvis, and womb. Thank them for everything they are doing for you and your baby.
- Continue moving through each part of your body, thanking it for what it does, and sending it love and breath.
- Experience gratitude and love for your body's ability to create and give life.
- Sit with this love for your body for as long as you would like.

Prenatal Worry and Anxiety

Is it just me, or do those two little lines on the pregnancy test increase your capacity for anxiety and worry tenfold? Not only are you worried about the precious little life that is growing inside of you, you're also worried about how this experience will impact you, what it means for the future, and a million other not-so-little things.

I worried a lot when I was pregnant. Every small little change in my body, or anything that seemed slightly out of the ordinary had me worried about the little guy. I even woke up in the middle of the night toward the end of my pregnancy terrified that our dog would decide she didn't want to be a big sister and that maybe she would think we didn't love her anymore because we had a baby. These are the types of things that would keep me up at night! There is so much change happening during this time, and the future is unknown. It can be hard not to worry.

Meditation can wire the brain to decrease anxiety, as discussed in the Meditation and Your Brain section (page 16). It can also help quiet the noise and constant mental chatter that happens during times of stress.

When you find these moments of worry and anxiety creeping in during your pregnancy, use this meditation to bring yourself back to center and slow down the swirling thoughts in your mind.

Guided Practice

- Begin this meditation by checking in with how you're feeling and what is happening in your body, mind, and heart.
- Let yourself feel whatever you are feeling.
- Begin the balancing breath.
- As you breathe, imagine you are bringing in peace of mind on the inhale and you are releasing stress and worry on the exhale.
- With each exhale, feel yourself release a tiny bit of your worry and anxiety.
- Repeat the following mantras three times each:
    - I am free from worry and stress.
    - I am filled with peace.
    - My mind is clear and I can manage what comes my way.
- Do this practice for at least four minutes.

Prenatal Insomnia

Everyone tells you that once baby is born, you'll never sleep again. What they fail to mention is that by that point, you've probably been experiencing sleepless nights for months. There's no shortage of reasons you can't get a good night's sleep when you're pregnant: heartburn, worry, you can't get comfortable, there is a human using your bladder as a pillow or drop-kicking you in the diaphragm, or, my personal favorite, you need a snack.

There are a few theories as to why pregnancy leads to sleep disruption, including hormonal changes and physical discomfort. There's also a theory that at the end of your pregnancy your body is preparing you to sleep in shifts at night, as if the baby was already there.

No matter why you are up, or what is causing your insomnia, the fact of the matter is that it's annoying at best and detrimental to your well-being at worse. You are growing a human life, and you need sleep to do that. So next time you find yourself tossing and turning at night, give this meditation a try.

Guided Practice

- Take a few deep breaths, inhaling through the nose, and sighing out through the mouth. Reposition yourself however you need to get as comfortable as possible.

- Tell yourself three times: *Now is the time for rest. I give myself permission to sleep.*

- Bring your awareness to baby. Give your baby bump a gentle little hug and tell your baby it is time for you to sleep and if baby is moving around, that's okay.

- Begin the relaxation breath.

- As you continue to breathe, move through each part of your body and let it fall asleep.

- Starting with your feet, slowly move through each part of your body, allowing it to unwind and fall asleep, bit by, on your exhales.

- Repeat this with your entire body.

- When you've finished your body scan, continue to breathe with long exhales until you drift off.

Breathe with Baby

Every woman will have a different experience when it comes to connecting with their babies. For some women it comes quickly, and they instantly feel a connection and bond to the little one growing inside them. For others, it might take a while. There is no right or wrong way to feel about pregnancy. For many of us, we may struggle to feel connected to the baby when they are still small and you can't yet feel their movements.

When I was pregnant, I felt differently each day. Some days my heart was ready to burst with love; some days I was scared out of my mind about the fact I was going to be a mother; and some days I was just resentful that this little guy had kept me up all night with my head in the toilet. Although I had many ups and downs emotionally during my pregnancy, I often found myself thinking of him and thinking that we were doing this together. Each morning when I sat quietly to meditate with him, I found that using my breath was one of the best tools I had to connect with my baby through meditation. I felt breathing together brought us closer.

The following meditation is the practice I started most of my days with when I was pregnant to connect with the little one within me.

Guided Practice

- Take a moment to get comfortable and settle in, making sure your spine is long, your diaphragm is uninhibited.
- Take your hands to your belly and connect with your baby.
- Feel the natural rhythm of your inhales and exhales.
- As you breathe, send the breath all the way down to your baby.
- Imagine your breath going down into your belly and surrounding your baby with nourishment and love.
- See the two of you breathing together, sharing love and nourishment with each breath, two bodies synched together.
- Sit, breathe, surround you baby with love and nourishment, and enjoy this time to breathe together.
- Stay here for as long as you would like.

Manifest a Healthy Pregnancy

You may be familiar with the idea of manifestation: that your thoughts have power, and if you think positively, you can bring change into your life. While there is a lot of evidence that backs up the theory of positive thinking, we often associate it with love or money. But there's no reason you can't apply the same manifestation logic during the prenatal stage.

Manifestation and positive thought can also be quite soothing during times of uncertainty and stress. Taking a few moments to clear your mind and think about what a healthy pregnancy would look and feel like can bring optimism and stress relief to your day.

If you find yourself worrying in between scans and wanting to manifest a healthy and happy pregnancy, use this guided meditation.

Guided Practice

- Take moment to get comfortable, relaxing your body. Get cozy and set your intention for what you are manifesting.
- State your intention clearly in your mind.
- Scan through your body and notice any areas where you are holding on to tension. Soften these spaces.
- Tune in to your energy and how you're feeling.
- Begin to raise your vibration by welcoming in positivity, gratitude, and nourishment from the world around you.
- In your mind's eye, visualize what a healthy pregnancy would look like for you, reflecting on how you would feel, what it would look like, and what the experience of a healthy pregnancy would be like for you and your baby during this time.
- Sit with your visualization, watching your healthy pregnancy play out in your mind's eye.
- When you are done with your visualization, state your intention once more.
- Close your meditation by trusting that it will come true. Thank the universe for giving you what you need for this healthy pregnancy.

Preparing for Labor and Delivery

Labor and delivery is something that can bring worry and anxiety to even the most seasoned mothers. There are so many unknowns, each labor and delivery is different, and let's be honest, it is hard! Bringing life into this world is no easy task, no matter how you do it. I had a lot of anxiety around labor and delivery, but eventually I decided that my birth plan didn't matter. Porkchop would arrive the way he was supposed to, and I would find out what that was when it happened.

For me, letting go of my attachment to a certain kind of birth felt freeing, but for you it might be different. And that's okay!

Just like an athlete uses meditation and guided visualization to prepare for a big game, no matter what kind of delivery you are hoping for, using meditation to mentally prepare yourself for labor is one of the best tools that you can use. When you are ready to start preparing for that big day, use this meditation as many times as you need to visualize your delivery the way you want it happen, and bring you some peace of mind as the day draws nearer.

Guided Practice

- Come to a comfortable place, quiet your mind, and relax your body.
- Check in with your body. When you think of labor and delivery, what comes up for you?
- Follow your breath, and welcome in thoughts and feelings as they come during this meditation.
- Begin to visualize your ideal labor. What does it look like? What does it feel like? Watch this play out in your mind in a positive, detailed way.
- Stick with your breath as you visualize your labor. See yourself breathing through contractions and labor happening in the ideal way for you.
- Now visualize your delivery: How it is? What happens? Watch this play out in your mind until the point where you are holding your baby in your arms, smiling down at them.
- Close your meditation by sending love and gratitude to your body, and trust that your labor and delivery will happen the way it is supposed to.

Forty Mantras for Mama

For Your Body

- (*inhale*) Nourishment. (*exhale*) Discomfort.
- I trust my body knows what to do.
- My body is strong, and my mind is clear.
- My breath is a powerful tool that I use every day.
- I am gentle with myself and honor what my body needs.
- I accept the changes in my body.
- I honor what I feel in my body, mind, and heart.
- My baby is safe, loved, and cared for within my body.
- I know what is best for my body and my baby.
- I am prepared for the birth of my baby.
- I honor what my body needs during my pregnancy.
- I trust my body to give birth.
- My body and my baby will work together to give birth.
- My body is the perfect vessel for my baby to grow.
- My body grows my baby, and my heart sends it love.

For Your Mind

- (*inhale*) Trust. (*exhale*) Fear.
- I accept where I am today.
- I am powerful, I am strong, I can do challenging things.
- I set healthy boundaries and say no when I need to.
- Each day is a different day, and I am present for this day.
- Motherhood is a journey, and my path is clear.
- Every experience helps me grow.
- My baby and I are connected.
- I am present each day on this journey.
- My baby and I are growing together each day.
- I am exactly the mother my baby needs.
- My baby is happy and healthy, and so am I.

For Your Heart

- I love my baby, and my baby loves me.
- Unconditional love pours through me.
- I honor the mother I am becoming.
- I am connected to my mother's intuition; I know what is best for my child.
- I give myself permission to rest.
- My heart is filled with an abundance of love for myself and my child.
- I am a loving and compassionate mother.
- Accepting help from others is easy for me.
- Motherhood comes to me with ease.
- I release my need for perfection.
- I am surrounded by love and support.
- I have everything I need within me to be a great mother.

CH 5

Meditations
for a Loving
Partnership

When you first think of meditation, you may think of it as a solo endeavor, a way for you to carve out a little bit of time to care for yourself and honor what is happening within you and around you. Although meditation can absolutely be that, you can also share this practice with a partner.

This chapter includes seven guided practices that you can do on your own or with your partner to help build a strong emotional foundation between the two of you as you walk the path of parenthood together. Carving out time to meditate with one another can contribute to your self-care as individuals while also fostering closeness in your relationship.

Everyone told me that when you have a child, your relationship with your partner changes. I don't think I fully listened. Rather, I didn't fully understand how becoming parents can change the dynamic of a relationship. My husband and I were both so happy and excited to welcome Porkchop into the world, and I couldn't ask for a better co-parent. But it would be a lie to say that parenthood didn't change us. Suddenly we were working like teammates rather than partners.

Those small moments of excitement, spontaneity, intimacy, and relationship maintenance that we had prioritized before having a baby were replaced with quick conversations about how the baby was doing, which family members were coming to visit, and what we should feed Porkchop for dinner.

This was our first foray into parenthood, and we worked so well together at it that we forgot our first role to one another as partners. I found that without making the conscious effort to prioritize time together through small acts like meditation, clear communication, and uninterrupted listening, falling out of lockstep with one another became easy.

The following meditations explore some of the struggles I have either personally experienced or heard about from other parents as they struggle to navigate parenthood with their partner. You can practice these meditations by yourself, or together with your partner, to help with clear communication, sparking intimacy, releasing resentment and expectation, practicing self-care, building boundaries, and taking time to return to one another.

Remember, you were a person before you were a partner, and you were a partner before you were a parent. Just as you take time for self-maintenance through daily meditation and self-care, taking a small amount of time each day to build a strong foundation of connection with your partner is a wonderful way to keep the health of your partnership alive and well.

A Meditation for Clear Communication

One of the most important things that partners need as they are raise tiny humans together is clear communication. You may find yourself talking to your partner all day about feeding schedules, diaper changes, daily routines, and everything else that goes into co-parenting. For me, when I was a new parent, I didn't find that outwardly communicating was the tricky part but instead struggled to feel heard and to practice active listening. Communication is a two-way street of listening and speaking. In those moments when you need a communication boost, or you are struggling with speaking or listening, use this meditation to clear and activate your throat chakra, the communication center of your energetic body.

Guided Practice

- Begin your meditation by finding a comfortable position.
- Take a big, deep breath in and sigh it out.
- Focus on the feeling of your throat clearing as you exhale and release.
- Do this three times.
- Settle into your natural breath pattern and keep your awareness on your throat.
- Visualize a blue cloud of mist at the throat center.
- See this mist clear and wash away any gunk, sluggishness, or other issues that may swirling around the throat, stopping you from speaking your truth, actively listening, or using your voice.
- Continue to visualize this cool, blue cloud of mist clearing your throat until you feel it has been cleared.
- Now visualize from your throat a golden cord of communication going from your throat to your partner's throat, opening up a clear and honest line of communication between the two of you.
- Visualize light moving back and forth along this cord.
- Take turns listening and speaking through your line of communication.

A Meditation to Boost Intimacy

When you become a parent, your priorities shift. Some of the things that used to feel important to us become less important when we prioritize what our baby needs. This is normal. However, it is too easy to let this temporary shift of priorities turn into a new normal, where you stay focused solely on your little one day in and day out and you forget about the need for intimacy with your partner.

When you feel you are losing your intimate connection with your partner and you want to re-ignite that spark, practice this meditation together.

Guided practice

- Begin this meditation by sitting close to one another, perhaps cross-legged with your knees touching, or lying next to one another and holding hands.
- Connect with your breath, breathe deeply, and release expectations.
- In your mind's eye, visualize a spark of desire igniting in your pelvis.
- See this spark begin to grow bigger and stronger with each breath.
- Watch this spark expand from your pelvis and spread throughout your entire body, until you are illuminated with this spark of desire.
- Focus on where your body is touching your partner's body and see your spark move into their body where it meets their spark, igniting your passion for one another where the sparks meet.
- Sit with these sparks of passion for a few minutes.
- Then sit up or open your eyes, look into one another's eyes closely and share three things that you love about your partner, and have your partner do the same for you.

Self-Care

It is a cliché, but it's true. You can't pour from an empty cup. This is true in parenthood and partnership. It's difficult to show up as your best self for those around you, including yourself, if you are being held together by threads.

Self-care is something that you hear about all the time. Images of bubble baths, pedicures, and glasses of wine come to mind, but self-care is so much more than that. Self-care is made up of small moments when you can hit the pause button and fill your cup up a little bit to keep it from running dry. Taking a full evening for self-care can be wonderful but so can finding five minutes of quiet time to just breathe or do a short meditation practice. Taking little bits of time during the day for your overall maintenance isn't a luxury but a necessity. Well-cared for parents and partners raise well-cared for children.

On days when you feel run ragged and you just need to hit the pause button, use this meditation.

Guided Practice

- Come to a quiet place, turn off all distractions, and if you need to, set a timer for ten minutes.

- Start your meditation by taking inventory of how you are doing and what are you feeling, thinking, and experiencing right now.

- Connect with your breath.

- Consciously slow down your breath and extend the inhales and exhales until your breath is low, slow, and controlled.

- Imagine you are lying under a starry sky with a full moon.

- As you lay under the stars and moon, let the moonlight and the twinkle of the stars reflect off your skin and fill you with cooling, calming energy.

- Lay, breathe, and be under the moonlight as you rest and reset.

Release Resentment Meditation

I have spent a large portion of my first years of motherhood navigating resentment. Not because my partner isn't an amazing partner—he is!—but, by default, sometimes things looked different for me as "mom" than they did for my partner. When I became a mother, everything changed. I no longer had the freedom to do whatever I wanted to do when I wanted to do it. I was up all hours of the night lugging my engorged boobs to a baby or a pump, I peed a little bit when I sneezed, and I was only able to take meetings during Porkchop's nap time or after he went to bed.

To say I never felt resentful of my partner who could wake up, take a shower, have breakfast, and go spend the day with adults, talking about things other than poop, breastmilk, wake windows, and swaddles would be a lie. Was it my partner's fault this was happening? No. Did that stop me from sometimes having the green-eyed monster creep in when I looked at how different our days had become since becoming parents? No.

Resentment happens. It can show up like a tiny crack in the sidewalk that you don't notice at first, but if you ignore it for too long the tiny crack can turn into a huge fissure that can break the sidewalk apart. Resentment can appear in different ways, so try to observe without judgment where you may be experiencing it and why.

Use this meditation in those moments when you find resentment taking hold and you want to work on releasing it.

Guided Practice

- Come to a comfortable position, close your eyes, and focus on your breath.
- Turn your palms upward toward the sky.
- In your mind's eye, visualize your heart center. See it and look at the resentment that is in your heart right now.
- Imagine a warm, golden, glowing light in your heart center begin to melt away and press the resentment from your heart.
- See this gold light pushing the resentment out of your heart, down your arms and out of your open palms, where it is removed from your heart and body.

- If you are practicing with your partner, after you have removed the resentment, hold hands and imagine gratitude pouring form your hands into their hands for several minutes.
- Close the meditation by sharing three things you appreciate your partner doing for you, and three ways they can help fulfill your needs today.

Releasing Expectations Meditation

Expectations aren't always a bad thing. Certain expectations in a relationship, such as respect, love, and showing up for one another, are bare bones expectations that should be fulfilled by our partner. The issue with expectations comes when you begin to create unrealistic expectations for who you partner is, what they can do, and how they should show up in your partnership.

When we become parents, we tend to have an idea in our head of what co-parenting *should* look like, or how we ourselves *should* look as a parent. And *should* is a slippery slope. What you should be doing or what your partner should be doing can quickly turn into what they are not doing and, ultimately, how they are coming up short. Going into situations with expectations can often set us up for disappointment.

Instead of leading with expectations, try leading with acceptance and clarity. Looking at yourself and your relationship with a clear, objective lens can help you release those expectations and instead see the situation for what it is.

Guided Practice

- Come to a comfortable position and settle in.
- Take three deep breaths in through the nose and out through the mouth.
- Settle into a natural rhythm of breath and focus on the rise and fall of the belly with each inhale and exhale.
- As you inhale, think *I accept my life as it is.*
- On the exhale, think *I release all expectations.*
- Continue to breathe and repeat these mantras for at least five minutes.

Return to One Another Meditation

During the process of becoming parents, there may times of drifting apart. You are both so focused on keeping this tiny little human (or humans) alive and everything else you do that finding time to connect and return to one another can be placed on the back burner.

For the first year and a half after Porkchop was born, we were both just focused on surviving, on learning how to be parents, and adapting to our new roles while also juggling careers, family, and friends that we began to drift away from one another.

Most nights I was so tired, overstimulated, touched out and over it, that once Porkchop was in bed, I went to bed just to be alone and get some rest, and I don't necessarily feel bad about this. I was doing the best I could with what I had, but I poured so much time and effort into one relationship and role that I had begun neglecting another.

Once we realized this was happening, we began doing small things to return to one another. It doesn't take a lot of time, and it doesn't have to be a big thing. But prioritizing a few minutes to be present and consciously return to one another and connect can be an extremely useful practice.

If you want to spend some time reconnecting with one another as partners, try doing this meditation together.

Guided Practice

- Come to a comfortable position and sit facing one another.
- Take three deep breaths.
- Allow your gaze to fall on your partner's eyes.
- Look deeply into your partner's eyes and try to see past the eye and into their heart and soul.
- Reflect on the beauty that is there and the person you decided to be in a partnership with.
- For five minutes, continue breathing slowly, looking deeply into each other's eyes and reflecting on the love you have for one another.
- When your time is up, take turns sharing something that you love, value, or appreciate about one another.

Building Boundaries

I know they say diamonds are a girl's best friend, but if we're being honest, it's boundaries. Nothing hurts the heart and soul quite like feeling like you are being taken advantage of, ignored, or disrespected. For many of us, creating and holding healthy boundaries can be extremely challenging, especially when it comes to your friends, family, and partner. But I want to clear something up right here and now: You are not a bad person for setting healthy, reasonable, and firm boundaries.

When you are working with someone to raise a child, it is essential that you both feel seen, heard, and respected. Creating boundaries is not only a way to share what you need and what you don't need, it is also a way to share mutual respect to your partner. Giving them a clear understanding of what you need and what you will accept gives them the opportunity to meet you where you are at and give you the love and respect you deserve.

If you are struggling to build boundaries in your life, try this meditation. Don't be too hard on yourself if it starts slow. Building boundaries can take time, and with continued practice it will become easier.

Guided Practice

- Come to a comfortable position and close your eyes.
- Begin your meditation by feeling your energy.
- Visualize your energy like a protective bubble all around you.
- Strengthen this bubble of energy, making it bright and strong.
- Continue to focus on the bubble of energy protecting you and repeat the following mantras as many times as you would like:
    - I set healthy and reasonable boundaries.
    - I am worthy of respect.
    - I honor myself by honoring my boundaries.
    - I am not afraid to stand up for what I need.
    - I clearly communicate my boundaries to my partner and family.

30 Mantras for Relationships

Mantras for the Self

- Communication comes easily to me.
- I have honest and realistic expectations.
- I communicate what I need to those around me.
- I am surrounded by love and support.
- Asking for help is a sign of strength.
- Laughter keeps my heart happy and light.
- Perfection is not expected.
- Love is unconditional.
- Each day I choose to respect and honor those I love.

Mantras for Your Partner

- I accept my partner for who they are, and they accept me.
- I embrace the flaws of myself and my partner.
- My partner sees me clearly.
- I listen to my partner's needs.
- Together we build a loving family.
- I am filled with gratitude for my partner.
- I take time to listen to my partner each day.
- I honor my partner's unique perspective.
- I am fulfilled and loved in my partnership.
- I ask for what I need.
- I show up for my partner daily.

Mantras About Partnership

- (inhale) Forgiveness. (exhale) Resentment.
- I support my partner, and they support me.
- My love is unconditional.
- I am fulfilled in my partnership.
- In my home, love is given and received in abundance.
- I prioritize moments to connect with my partner.
- My partnership is filled with respect.
- Each day is a chance to work together and live with respect.
- My partnership does not define me.
- I am not alone on my path of parenthood.

Conclusion

If you have made it this far, thank you. Thank you for letting me share what I love in such a personal and vulnerable way. Learning how to incorporate mindfulness and meditation into my life and using these tools as part of my parental toolbox was often the life raft that kept me afloat during those first few years of motherhood.

There are so many things that I wish I could say to you about parenthood, how special you are, and what an amazing parent you are to your child. But I will leave you with this: No one in this world is a better parent to your children than you are. No matter how you found your way to parenthood, every day that you wake up, try your best, and love your little ones and yourself is a wonderful day. You are enough in this world and for your kids, and you always know what is best for you and your family. Trust your gut, open your heart, and let yourself be human.

References

Chapter 1

J. Brewer, P. Worhunsky, J. Gray, Yi-Yuan Tang, J. Weber, and H. Kober. *Meditation Experience Is Associated with Differences in Default Mode Network Activity and Connectivity.* Proceedings of the National Academy of Sciences, 2011.

Mayo Clinic staff. *Meditation: A Simple, Fast Way to Reduce Stress.* 2022.

Mengran Xu, Christine Purdon, Paul Seli and Daniel Smilek. Mindfulness and Mind Wandering: The Protective Effects of Brief Meditation in Anxious Individuals. *Consciousness and Cognition*, 2017 (May).

Pedro Mateos-Aparicio and Antonio Rodriguez-Moreno, "The Impact of Studying Brain Plasticity," *Frontiers in Cellular Neuroscience* (2019, February 27).

Sara Lazar. "How Meditation Can Reshape Our Brains," TEDxCambridge, 2011.

Chapter 2

Jill Anderson. *The Benefit of Family Mealtime.* Harvard Graduate School of Education, 2020.

Chapter 3

Alex M. Wood, Stephen Joseph, Joanna Lloyd and Samuel Atkins. Gratitude Influences Sleep Through the Mechanism of Pre-Sleep Cognitions. *Journal of Psychosomatic Research*, 2009 (January).

Amrisha Vaish, Tobias Grossmann, and Amanda Woodward. Not All Emotions Are Created Equal: The Negativity Bias in Social-Emotional Development. *Psychological Bulletin*, 2008 (May).

Dianna Quach, Kristen E. Jastrowki Mano, and Kristi Alexander. A Randomized Controlled Trial Examining the Effect of Mindfulness Meditation on Working Memory Capacity in Adolescents. *Journal of Adolescent Health*, 2016 (May).

Habib Yaribeygi, Yunes Panahi, Hedayat Sahraei, Thomas Johnston and Amirhossein Sahebkar. *The Impact of Stress on Body Function: A Review.* EXCLI Journal, 2017.

Hallie Lavine. "Meditation and Yoga for ADHD." WebMD, 2022.

Laura G. Kiken and Natalie J. Shook. Looking Up: Mindfulness Increases Positive Judgments and Reduces Negativity Bias. *Social Psychological and Personality Science*, 2011 (January 10).

Robby Berman. New Study Suggests We Have 6,200 Thoughts Every Day. *Big Think*, 2020 (July 16).

Robert A. Emmons. "The Psychology of Gratitude: An Introduction," in R. A. Emmons and M. E. McCullough (eds.), The Psychology of Gratitude (pp. 3–16). *Oxford University Press*, 2004.

Sara Lazar. "How Meditation Can Reshape Our Brains," TEDxCambridge, 2011.

Chapter 4

Anjulie Dhillon, Elizabeth Sparkes, and Rui V. Duarte. Mindfulness-Based Interventions During Pregnancy: A Systematic Review and Meta-analysis, *Mindfulness*, 2017.

Acknowledgments

I want to take a moment to thank. . .

My mom for giving me life, for teaching me how to dream, and for always being my biggest cheerleader. It's hard to put into words what you've done for me over the last thirty-two years, so I'll just leave it at thank you.

My husband, Ben, for being my partner in parenting and in life, and for holding my hand during the labor and delivery of this book and our baby.

The circle of women who surround me with love daily, help guide me through the ups and downs of motherhood, and are always there for me. You know who you are, and I am grateful every day that you are in my life.

About the Author

Kelly Smith is the founder of Yoga for You and the host of the iTunes chart-topping meditation podcast *Mindful in Minutes* and its prenatal spinoff *Meditation Mama*. She is an E-RYT 500, YACEP, and master trainer in meditation, yoga nidra, and restorative yoga. Her meditations and work have been featured in *Meditation Magazine*, Popsugar Fitness, ABC News, The Bump, Twin Cities Live, and the *Lavendaire Lifestyle Podcast*. She is also the author of *Mindful in Minutes: You Are Not Your Thoughts* She lives in Minneapolis with her family. You can find her on Instagram as @yogaforyouonline

Index